L. KEITH BROWN
ANTHROPOLOGY

D1226236

JAPANESE SOCIETY TODAY

Second Edition

TADASHI FUKUTAKE

UNIVERSITY OF TOKYO PRESS

©UNIVERSITY OF TOKYO PRESS, 1981

First Edition 1974, Second Edition 1981

All rights reserved. No part of this publication may be re-
produced or transmitted in any form or by any means,
electronic or mechanical, including photocopy, recording,
or any information storage and retrieval system, without
permission in writing from the publisher.

UTP Number 3036–57100–5149
ISBN 0–86008–291–1

Printed in Japan

JAPANESE SOCIETY TODAY

To
My Foreign Friends

Contents

List of Tables

Preface

When the first edition of this book was published in 1974, two years had passed since publication of the original Japanese edition. Thus it is now nearly ten years since I completed the original manuscript.

The reception given the book has been gratifying. It has been widely read as a basic introduction to contemporary Japanese society, and has been reprinted several times. However, as the statistics incorporated in the first edition were gathered around 1970, I have felt the necessity of updating them and revising the text in light of recent changes in various sectors of Japanese society, so that I can still claim to be describing "Japanese society today" in a literal sense.

The pressures of other work kept me for some time from the task of revision, and the book has as a result been unavailable. Still I have received from time to time letters from friends here and abroad asking for the book, and the publisher has also received queries from readers and bookstores. In the meantime, the result of the 1980 national census became available, and I finally made up my mind to devote all my energies to the task of revision.

The Japanese economy, which began to grow so rapidly in 1955, has shifted to a slow and steady type of growth, mainly due to the 1973 oil crisis, which was taking place at the time the first edition of this book was published. The post-oil crisis years have brought a number of significant political and economic changes: however, most of the basic social problems I discussed ten years ago are still with us. Regrettably, therefore, I have felt nearly no need to modify my overall view of Japanese society. I tried to incorporate the most recent statistical data and rewrote numerous parts of the book; but even so, the second edition is not different in substance from the first. I sincerely hope that the time will come when a critical study of Japanese society like this one will be out of date; but that time is not yet in sight.

Japan's "success story," mainly in terms of economics, has recently attracted the world's attention. On the one hand, Japan is considered by developing nations to be a model of industrialization to be emulated; on the other, severe criticism has come from the other advanced countries owing to recent trade friction. I fear that such praise and criticism are both based on more than a little misunderstanding—in other words, on superficial analyses of Japanese society. I would be satisfied if the present book, even in a minor way, could help to dispel mistaken ideas and promote and deepen understanding of Japanese society, past and present.

Tadashi Fukutake

Summer 1981

Preface to the First Edition

In writing this volume I have tried to present an overall view of modern Japanese society, giving as much information as possible in limited space about the recent history, problems, hopes and real prospects for this society. It has been by no means easy for a rural sociologist to tackle Japanese society as a whole, in its every aspect. I have undoubtedly failed to cover certain areas that some will deem important, but I have tried, above all, to avoid the specialist approach which so often produces a distorted impression of what our society is and how it works.

I was given a good opportunity to begin this book when, as a lecturer for sophomores at the University of Tokyo, I had to prepare a text on the basic sociology of modern Japan for use in the course. This volume is the outcome of that project. It was published in Japanese at the end of 1972, and although it is certainly not the definitive work on this subject, I am pleased that it has been widely read and has already had three printings.

In the preface to the Japanese edition, I wrote:

Having become painfully aware of the multi-faceted, deeplying problems facing Japanese society today, I wanted to attract the interest not only of my students, but of the concerned lay reader as well. I have tried to present data that will cause both academician and the general reader to think seriously about the future of our society and to reflect upon the problems that we face. It is with that basic purpose that this book was written.

Thus, I hoped to awaken the interest of readers in any occupation or profession and to stimulate their concern for problems that lie right at their doorstep. The appearance of the English edition also fulfills a hope of mine—the hope that foreign readers will have a chance to look at both the strengths and weaknesses of Japanese society within a general, balanced framework, and that their understanding of Japan and the Japanese may thereby deepen. There are available any number of fine works by Japanese authors on specific aspects of this society, some in English translation. Among them are Chie Nakane's *Japanese Society* (University of California Press, 1971), Takeshi Ishida's *Japanese Society* (Random House, Inc., 1971), and my own *Japanese Rural Society* (Oxford University Press, 1967). There remained, nonetheless, a lack of general works that placed specific aspects of society in an overall context. It is that need I hoped to fill, by giving sufficient information on all the basic aspects of this society and some suggestion about its implications to enable the reader to grasp, in the broad spectrum, how those parts fit together and affect each other.

I believe that positive understanding by non-Japanese of Japanese society is important for our nation as a whole, and that we can benefit by constructive criticism from those who stand outside but understand our problems. A true friend is one who will look critically and try to help positively, knowing both one's good and bad points.

It may appear that I overemphasize shortcomings at the expense of assets in this book, but it seems that the problems we face are truly overwhelming. It will require not only the efforts of Japanese but the understanding, encouragement and help of others as well to solve these problems. The views expressed here are of course only my own, recorded with the hope and expectation that our society can and will begin to move in more balanced, human and stable directions.

I am indebted to Shigeo Minowa, director of the University of Tokyo Press, for his encouragement and assistance in making this English edition a reality. Translation was undertaken by the staff of *The Japan Interpreter* under the direction of its editor, Tsutomu Kano.

Tadashi Fukutake

Summer 1973

JAPANESE SOCIETY TODAY

Introduction: Modern Japanese Society

1. The Concept of "Society"

Less than a hundred years have passed since the term *shakai* came into the Japanese language. It was first used in the early years of the Meiji period to mean "society." The very lack of terminology to convey the idea of "society" clearly bespeaks the conditions of a century ago: Japan was not a modern society.

In Europe, too, the word "society" came into general use along with the growth of the modern bourgeoisie. Under the feudal order there was little reason for people to be aware of any broader social fabric outside of the town or village in which they were born and raised, and where they lived and died. The breakdown of the feudal system, however, eased communal and hierarchical restrictions on social mobility, and the development of the capitalist economy and advances in transportation and communication technology broadened the scope of social life. Only then did people become truly aware of a wider human community that extended beyond their own towns. A modern citizenry and civil society thus came into being.

In Japan, however, modern society could not develop in the same manner toward what we think of as a typical civil society. From the first, Meiji government policies promoted industrialization and greater production, national wealth, and military strength; consequently, Japan's capitalist economy began to grow at a remarkable rate. That this growth was protected and fostered from the very beginning by the national government meant that no truly liberal tradition developed with it. Public education, too,

3

was rapidly promoted on a nationwide scale, using as a foundation the kind of education developed in the Tokugawa period temple schools. Education was instrumental in producing a modern industrial labor force; this should be noted as one of the factors in the rapid growth of a capitalist economy in Japan. On the other hand, because this education emphasized moral training in the Confucian virtues of filial piety and loyalty, it did not instill any broad understanding of society.

The tradition of the early Meiji period centered on the goal of acquiring Western techniques while fostering the "Japanese spirit" (*wakon yōsai*), and its simultaneous emphasis on the virtues of the East and the science and technology of the West distorted modernization to favor economic development and military expansion. It did not produce a citizenry who could see this distortion and seek a balance between social and economic development.

Moreover, the word "society," interposed between "family" and "nation," conveyed a sense of threat to both. "Society" (and "social") tended to be associated with "socialism" and carried a connotation which seemed incompatible with Japan's characteristic family system and unique national polity. This feeling reached a peak of fervor during Word War II, when total mobilization for the war effort pushed "society" and "social" into the category of taboo terms. (For example, "social work" had to be rephrased as "welfare work.") The propensity to neglect, even shun, the word and the concept of "society" symbolized the conditions that allowed the incursion of Japanese imperialism into other countries. The development of the Japanese economy suffered a setback during the wartime period, thus revealing the weaknesses in the structure of Japanese society. It was not until after the collapse of Japanese imperialism that the country first set foot on the road to a genuine modern civil society.

This new road could be seen in the shift from training in morals and civic duties to education in the social studies. The old traditions were so deep-rooted, however, that they survived even the extraordinary experience of total defeat. Under the direction of the Occupation forces, many policies to democratize Japan's institutions were put into effect, some with truly positive results. But the inescapable weakness of all of them was that these were "handed-down democracy." The main emphasis of the Occupation policy later moved from experiments in democratization to the formation of an anticommunist base in Japan, and changes were promoted ostensibly to rectify the "excesses" of democratization and to adapt the Occupation reforms to the actual Japanese situation.

After the war Japan ceased to be a military power, thus abandoning half of its twofold prewar goal, *fukoku kyōhei* (wealthy nation and strong army). Following a period of reconstruction and recovery, however, national policy was turned to building up an extraordinarily high rate of economic growth and a "wealthy nation." In the course of this effort the original goal of democratization was soon buried in oblivion.

The lag of social development behind the economy has produced an imbalance even more marked during the past ten-odd years. Japanese society, having supported such disproportionate economic growth, does not yet have firmly rooted democratic institutions. It is not entirely impossible then that as Japan continues to pursue the goal of enriching itself it may again seek the status of a military power.

Perhaps there will be no return to prewar patterns, when "society" was dangerous word, but if Japan should again choose the course of military power, its civil society, shaky as it is, may be subjected to an intolerable strain. The Japanese "miracle" of becoming a great economic power has by now proven to be a disaster, as the growing seriousness of the pollution problem and the setback of growth after the 1973 oil crisis clearly indicate. People are beginning to question their optimistic faith in the wisdom of the steady increases in the GNP which took place all through the sixties. In recent years, the call for a change in direction has become louder. It is not at all clear whether these voices will effect any change in the nation's priorities. The structure of society and popular social awareness are, in fact, much weaker than the economic structure and consciousness. Society itself has yet to be given adequate recognition. It is no easy matter for such a society, dominated by the economy, to change the course of government so as to balance civil and political institutions within the society. Nevertheless, efforts in this direction must be intensified, not abandoned. Unless social problems are given precedence over economic, the many ills that present-day Japan suffers cannot be cured.

2.   An Outline of the Social Structure

Before proceeding with an analysis of the problems of contemporary Japan, I would like to outline the prewar social structure of Japan and describe roughly how it has changed since the war.

In the first years of Meiji, over 80 percent of the total population was agrarian, and the urban population (those living in cities or towns of over 10,000) amounted to less than 10 percent. Later, however, the development of modern industry attracted more people to the cities, and there was a gradual increase in the urban population. The concentration of people in the cities became especially notable after World War I, then became even greater after the world-wide depression of the early thirties. Growing militarism and preparation for war prompted the expansion of the heavy and chemical industries, and by the last years of World War II the urban population was reaching over 40 percent.

After the Meiji period, industrialization meant the establishment of new industrial cities, and this also contributed to urban concentration of the population. On the other hand, many Japanese cities, originally castle towns of feudal lords, retained their feudalistic character as they underwent modern adaptations. So, though the physical and material aspects of growth were creating an urban society, a deeply communal character remained in the social structure of Japanese cities. The people who flowed into the large cities were not transformed into modern citizens but retained their ties with the rural areas from which they came.

The rural districts entered the modern age even before emancipation of the peasantry was completed. Following the Meiji Restoration, annual tributes required during the feudal era were replaced by a cash land tax, which subjected Japanese farmers to the stresses of a capitalist money economy. One result was a rapid differentiation of classes. Owner-tenant cultivators and tenant farmers each accounted for about one-third of all farm households. Tenant farming comprised 70 percent of all farming. Thus, the Japanese peasantry soon became the object of exploitation by a small number of landlords. The rule of primogeniture also operated to siphon off younger sons, who then became a source of urban industrial labor. The number of farm households (about 5.5

million) and the farming population (about 14 million) did not undergo much change from the Meiji period up to World War II. Population increase occurred only in those areas where people were drawn off into other industries or to the cities. Thus, the premodern character of Japanese rural communities was bound to survive for a long time.

This situation changed dramatically after the war. Devastated cities were rapidly rebuilt and the economy began its dramatic upswing in the mid-fifties. Recent economic growth has brought with it urban concentration of the population on an unprecedented scale. During the immediate postwar period, when food was scarce the land reform may have helped the rural districts to achieve temporarily better living conditions than the cities. Thereafter, the picture changed as the gap between industry and agriculture widened in terms of income and productivity. The rural communities began to look quite different from the prewar period. Population growth in the cities, too, developed in an unbalanced surge, inundating the already crowded industrial belt along the western Pacific side of the country with more people. The geographic imbalance of modern industry has gone beyond easy rectification, despite the promotion of regional development plans and visions of new industrial cities. The nation has been divided into prefectures which are losing population and cities and prefectures which are becoming extremely overpopulated. Even in prefectures where the population is declining, the central cities are expanding, creating population imbalances not only on the national but also on the local level. Finally, the megalopolises around a few excessively large cities and their suburbs (especially Tokyo) are virtually being choked by overpopulation and severe urban problems of every kind.

In contrast, agricultural population, depleted by other industries during the past decade, now amounts to no more than 10 percent of the employed population. The exodus to the cities has consisted mainly of young men and male workers in their prime, thus resulting in a relatively higher average age level of the farm labor force and a higher proportion of women in it; the number of farm households with secondary occupations has also increased. Agriculture and the rural villages are steadily growing more desolate as their residents leave or die without successors. Since daily commuting to an industrial job from a farm community is often impossible in underdeveloped areas, long stays away from home for such work have become common. In many mountain village regions whole families have left a village, with the result that the village, unable to maintain its community life, has broken up. While concentration in the cities has created serious overcrowding, populations in farm and mountain village regions have become too sparse for survival.

In addition to the regional structure of Japanese society that we have been discussing, let us consider the prewar social class structure and how it has changed. The Meiji government quickly abolished the warrior-peasant-artisan-merchant status hierarchy and decreed a new system in which the four classes were legally equal. This opened, to a certain extent, new channels for social mobility, providing a necessary condition for the development of modern industry. However, the traditional status-consciousness survived long afterwards. The persistence of such consciousness even after the dissolution of the feudal class system served to stimulate people's desires to rise in the world. Efforts to move up the social ladder proved to be vitally important and operated to fuel the development of the economy. At the same time, it is significant that this precipitous pursuit of growth greatly undermined the trend toward a more egalitarian class structure.

The ruling upper classes before the war consisted roughly of the wealthy capitalist class, large landowners and politicians and high-level officials. Their position was secure, supported as it was by the emperor system. Linked with this group were such medium- and small-sized entrepreneurs as the owners of small factories and large stores, who, with medium- and small-sized landowners, formed a small middle class directly above the peasants, laborers, small merchants, and artisans. The new middle class of public officials, white-collar workers in large enterprises, teachers and other professional workers was not only smaller in number than the old middle class but also fully incorporated into the overall structure of social stratification. In fact, the new middle class played the role of intermediary between the ruling class and the old middle class.

Thus, prewar Japanese society was run according to the will of the upper class, which had behind it the authority of the emperor. Farmers' unions had proven totally unable to assert themselves, and powerful labor unions were not allowed to exist. It was very difficult, indeed, for the lower classes to put up any resistance to unfair policies. The great mass of the lower classes lived in unchanging conditions of poverty; they could compensate for their inferior status, however, by feeling superior to those below them, those at the very bottom of the social ladder. But even these people at the lowest stratum of the imperial hierarchy could gain emotional satisfaction by identifying themselves as the "poor," the "true" children of the emperor.

This class structure was modified considerably after the war. No essential change took place in the character of the ruling class, but the emperor system, its firm support, did change. The prewar political scene was completely dominated by the conservatives, although a degree of political party rivalry was permitted to develop. The postwar scene was quite different. Of those belonging to the former middle class, the landlords were ruined by the land reform. Growing industrialization strengthened the new middle class. The middle class's domination of the lower classes was weakened, and within the lower classes the position of the workers rose. Through the organization of trade unions the political sympathies of the workers were channeled to the reform parties. The conservatives still continued to predominate in politics and the economy but in the national political arena at least a third or more threw their support to the forces of reform. This shift was one of the results of change in the class structure.

However, the reform forces, which now constitute over one-third of the Diet, became increasingly weak, as one can see by examining the political lineup of the nation, beginning with the prefectures and moving down to the cities, towns and villages. In local government, in most cases, even though there have been increases in the number of self-government bodies controlled by reform forces in recent years, rigid conservative rule still holds sway. The national government, too, is controlled by the power of large-scale capital; it did not turn out to be a government *for* the people. Economic growth is established as the primary goal; the dictates of capital needs have been given priority over popular and social welfare. In other words, the prevailing logic is that if the pie is to be divided among the people, it must first be made larger, and until that is accomplished, the lower-class masses should endure their poverty.

3. Today's Japan and Problems of the Future

The prevalence of this kind of logic has lifted Japan to second place in GNP among noncommunist nations and to third in the world behind the United States and the USSR. Japan has become an economic superpower, but the fact remains that it is occupying only fifteenth place in per capita national income. If we consider what it has cost to rise to third place in GNP, and the scarcity of stock accumulated in the economy until now, ours cannot be said to be a truly wealthy country. It may have the world's third biggest GNP, but the well-being of the people, which cannot be measured in economic terms, would be rated far lower than the fifteenth place Japan occupies in per capita national income.

Japan still stands midway between the advanced countries and the developing nations, combining aspects of both. Here is one of the greatest industrial capacities in the world, rooted in a system that permits inadequate wages (though nominal wages are steadily rising), little or no provision for improving the quality of the environment, and the low level of social security deriving from immaturity. A variety of electrical appliances crowded into small living quarters, television sets in numbers exceeded only by America—this typifies modern Japan.

The past ten or more years of booming growth, industrialization and urbanization have affected all communities and all classes of society. The traditional social framework of local communities and small groups has been further weakened, accompanied by the breakdown of group sanctions and the steady dispersion of individuals. This development is typical of conditions in a growing mass society.

A capitalist society based on mechanized mass production injects the individual into a process of increasingly specialized division of labor. He becomes a tiny cog in a vast bureaucratic organization and loses his sense of individual identity. The impersonal social relationships in such a mechanized society make him feel isolated and lonely. He sees himself as just part of a nameless mass that has lost any friendly intimacy and security. This tendency could be seen among some of the white-collar class even before the war, but on the whole, familial relations and the sense of community in the local society held it in check. But now family ties have been weakened and community structures broken up, and the difference between blue- and white-collar workers has decreased. At the same time the new middle class has been steadily growing, to produce more evidence of a typical mass society.

Generally speaking, Japan does not have a tradition of asceticism comparable to the Protestant ethic, and money assiduously saved is lavishly spent all at once on ceremonial occasions. These include comings-of-age, weddings, funerals, ceremonies for the deceased, local Shinto shrine festivals and seasonal celebrations. Conditions of mass society have made such occasions more common and everyday affairs. Large-scale mass amusement is provided by commercial, profit-making enterprises to satisfy the demand, and it is promoted through mass media advertising. Supported by the growth of the economy and encouraged by TV and other advertising displays, consumption levels are being pushed steadily upward. Hence we see many people impelled to buy a car for leisure use on their days off, while they are virtually forced to live in tiny, cramped quarters in, for example, a public housing development.

Such a combination of inadequate public housing and private-car ownership epitomizes the average situation in modern Japanese society. It is impossible to build a consumer culture that provides security for people in old age if the average employee cannot buy a home even if he spends all his retirement pay. Today's values have turned sharply toward *maihōmushugi* ("my-home-ism"), which implies concern for one's own family first, and satisfaction of immediate desires rather than planning for the future. So people at lower wage levels, pursuing the satisfaction of momentary cravings, seek temporary escape from the realities of life in some form of gambling such as bicycle races, or in other amusements. This kind of lack of alternatives cannot produce a sound or healthy society.

It is vital that the nation's per capita income be raised and that the national welfare rise accordingly, instead of everyone only trying to push up the GNP. We can expect Japan to further sustain its economic growth, though not at the high level of the sixties, and to progress as a society noted for its high productivity. But if national policy continues to place primary importance on economic development, the imbalance in society will not be cured. On the surface Japan's prosperity would appear even more striking, but the same problems that we see today would remain, together with the growth of new kinds of social deprivation. Japan's social ailments reflect what is called a dual structure of the economy and the underdeveloped social security system. Thus, instead of making the "pie" larger, more emphasis must be given to equitable allocation, or the cracks in society will become wider and wider.

The challenge for this period is to create a balance between social and economic development in the immediate future. The concept of social development, as will be explained in detail later, originated in connection with the modernization of developing countries. But ever since the Meiji period social development in Japan has been sacrificed to the continuous pursuit of economic growth. The following are key points in any effort to eliminate the resulting gap.

First, although it is late now, a proper living environment must be created. There has been a sharp increase in the investment of social capital in production, but such investment has always been at the expense of investment in higher standards of living. Some reforms, although very few, have been made in recent years as an overflow of the economic growth, but the investment in living environment is still very poor. The limited living environment itself has been a source of many current social problems, exacerbated by the delay in trying to improve conditions.

Second, the actual level of social security must be raised. All kinds of "social security" measures have been tried in recent years and the official standard has been raised, but as the welfare programs lack depth, their actual level is still very low. Taking into consideration the fact that the society is rapidly becoming old-aged, the demand for a well-organized and adequate social security system has become even stronger. Healthy economic development depends on action now to divide the pie equally, as quickly as possible and among as many people as possible. As long as conditions remain unchanged, the deep-seated pathological conditions in urban life will not disappear, nor will the insecurity of rural society be eliminated.

Third, social development requires new investment in education. Education has been of crucial importance, as attested by the fact that Japan alone, of all the countries in Asia, has achieved exceptional economic development. But for this society to develop to a point where it is worthy to be called a "culturally advanced nation," there must be a return to the original aims of the early Meiji years and a renewed emphasis on education. That over 94 percent of Japanese students go on to high school education and that there are over 960 universities and colleges including junior colleges—these facts are no guarantee of the positive development of education. They represent the minimum investments required to maintain education at its present level. Adequate provision of education beyond this must be carried out to insure real equality of opportunity.

If Japan were to move in this direction—if Article 25 of the Constitution ("Every citizen has the right to live a healthy and cultured life") were fully realized—many of Japan's problems could be adequately tackled. It would also be possible to improve social conditions while promoting further development. Dialogue between the conservatives and reformists, now so widely split, would then have a sound basis on which to begin again. In addition, a new democratic unity of national interest would probably arise. The Japanese are now at the crossroads; the road we take from now on will determine whether or not the brilliant prospects for our society toward the twenty-first century will be realized.

I. Population and Social Structure

1. Demographic Change

The population of Japan at the time of the Meiji Restoration was about 34 million. It began to grow quickly thereafter, when the restrictions on population growth of the Tokugawa period were removed. In 1911, as the Meiji period gave way to the Taishō, the total population exceeded 50 million. It had reached 70 million by the beginning of World War II. As a resource-poor land Japan might indeed have seemed to rank with the "have-nots." Such reasoning became justification for confronting the "have" nations and invading those weaker than Japan. The policy of encouraging population growth required by the aggressive nature of the war meant that this level of population was maintained throughout the long period of World War II.

Japan's population of 72 million in 1945 reached 80 million by 1948 as a result of the so-called baby boom and the repatriation of soldiers and others who had been abroad. For the country as a whole, the loss of colonies and the limited opportunity to emigrate caused population growth to be regarded with concern. Nevertheless, as is usual in the aftermath of a war, the birth rate rose sharply; coupled with a decrease in the death rate, it led to a rapid increase in population.

To limit population increase, the government greatly modified the Eugenic Protection Law in 1952, loosening restrictions on abortion. Thereafter the birth rate gradually declined, and since 1955 it has remained below 20 per thousand. But the death rate has also declined, so that the natural increase has continued to be about 10 per thousand, with lower figures during some years. In 1956 the population rose to 90 million; ten

14

years later, in 1967, it reached the 100–million mark; and the 1980 census recorded 117 million.

Japan is now the seventh most populous country in the world. But its population density of 314 per square kilometer ranks it fifth, behind only Bangladesh, Korea, Holland, and Belgium. If one subtracts Japan's mountainous regions, the density of population in the nonmountainous areas is much higher than that in the countries of western Europe. Japan is still an overpopulated country.

Table 1.   Total Population and Population Density

	Population (in ten thousands)	Density (sq. km.)
1872	3,481	91
1900	4,385	115
1920	5,596	147
1930	6,445	169
1940	7,193	188
1945	7,215	196
1950	8,412	226
1955	9,008	242
1960	9,430	253
1965	9,921	266
1970	10,467	281
1975	11,194	301
1980	11,706	314

Awareness of the problem of overpopulation resulted in rapid curtailment of births after the postwar baby boom. Between 1956 and 1964 the annual net reproduction rate of the female population was less than one; then it turned upward, but since 1975 it has been less than one again; this rate is not enough to maintain the existing population. Abortions played a large part in this extreme reduction in births. According to some estimates of birth prevention, in 1955 the ratio of birth control use to abortions was 4 to 6. It is estimated that this ratio changed to 6 to 4 in 1960 and 7 to 3 in 1965. But the birth rate rose again, and from 1965 to 1974 consecutively it exceeded 18 per thousand, except for an unusual

Table 2.   Population Trends (per thousand)

	Birth rate	Death rate	Rate of natural increase
1940–43	30.7	16.3	14.4
1947	34.3	14.6	18.7
1950	28.1	10.9	17.2
1955	19.4	7.8	11.6
1960	17.2	7.6	9.6
1965	18.6	7.1	11.4
1970	18.8	6.9	11.8
1975	17.1	6.3	10.8
1980	13.6	6.2	7.3

drop in 1966, the year of *hinoe uma* (occurring every sixty years and considered an inauspicious year for the birth of female children). However, since 1975 it has decreased year by year; it dropped to less than 15 per thousand in 1978, and the birth rate in 1980 was lower than that of 1966, the lowest on record.

Some maintain that before the war children were considered treasures, and, though costly to feed, each was regarded as potential support in old age; but that after the war children were weighed against durable consumer goods, and the rise in consumer demand often meant an increase in birth control. At any rate,

Table 3.   Percentages of Population by Age Group, with Projections for the Future

	–14	15–64	65–	15–59	60–
1920	36.5	58.3	5.3	55.3	8.2
1930	36.6	58.7	4.8	56.0	7.4
1940	36.1	59.2	4.7	56.2	7.8
1950	35.4	59.6	4.9	56.9	7.7
1960	30.2	64.1	5.7	61.1	8.9
1970	24.0	68.9	7.1	65.4	10.7
1980	23.5	67.4	9.0	63.5	12.9
1990	21.0	68.0	11.0	62.8	16.3
2000	20.2	65.6	14.3	60.0	20.0

since the number of children which parents want to have does not seem likely to change from the present two, the birth rate is expected to remain at about this level from now on.

In any case, the low birth and death rates of about 14 and 6 per thousand, respectively, point to the attainment of a stability in vital statistics comparable to that of western Europe. However, even if this means that Japan's future is to some degree free from the problem of overpopulation, it must also handle the problems of a reduction in the labor force and an increase in the aged population.

At the present time the proportion of people 65 years of age or older is 9 percent. Twenty years from now, as we enter the twenty-first century, it will be nearly twice that—14 percent or more, as can be seen from the figures in Table 3. With the remarkable increase in the average life expectancy (it is now age 73.5 for men, 78.9 for women), the problem of the aged, coupled as it is with changes in the structure and nature of the family, will not be an easy one to solve in the future.

While the number of the aged has increased, there has been a decline in the labor force, which must support the former. The number of people in the productive years between 15 and 64 was about 50 million in 1950, 60 million in 1960, over 70 million in 1970 and 79 million in 1980 as the baby boom population reached maturity and joined the labor force. However, the working population of 44 million in 1960 increased only 13 million to 57 million in 1980 because the larger proportion of youths continuing to high school and college resulted in fewer applicants for jobs upon graduation from junior high or high school. Fifteen years ago, of males aged 15 to 24 not quite 30 percent were in school, and of females only 25 percent. But today more than half of the males and nearly half of the females in the same age group are in school. This trend will probably increase from now on. High school attendance has become almost compulsory, and greater numbers of students are going on to university. How will this affect the structure of the labor force? Will the quantity and quality of labor be adequate to meet contemporary demands? These questions, and the problem of providing security for the aged, pose enormous problems for Japanese society.

2. Regional Distribution

Most of the 34 million people of early Meiji times lived in the rural districts. In 1878 there were 99 towns and cities with populations of 10,000 or more; their share of the total population amounted to only 9.8 percent. Twenty years later, in 1898, there were 166 such towns and cities, embracing 15.8 percent of the population. The first national census in 1920 gave these figures as 232 and 36.1 percent, respectively.

Before towns and villages began to be amalgamated in 1953, urban and rural populations were generally expressed as city district (*shibu*) and country district (*gunbu*) populations. By 1940 the proportion of the former had risen to 38.0 percent, from 18.1 percent in 1920.

During World War II this concentration of people in the cities temporarily decreased because of a reverse flow into the country. But by the time reconstruction was completed a return to the prewar situation had taken place. During the mid-fifties, when town and village mergers took place on a nationwide scale, urban concentration reached a level comparable to the prewar high. Massive urban immigration continued until about 1960, especially into the large metropolitan areas. In the ten years between 1950 and 1960 the population of the six largest cities increased by 50 percent, or 5.48 million, and their proportion of the total population rose from 13.5 to 17.9 percent.

In the next five years, however, we find that while Tokyo, Yokohama and Nagoya continued to expand, rates of population increase declined in Osaka, Kyoto and Kobe. And in the past ten years all except Yokohama have shown slightly decreasing levels of concentration; even in Tokyo and Osaka, it is showing a gradual decrease. That is, although the percentage of their populations rose to 18.7 of the national total in 1965, by 1970 it had decreased to 18.2, and by 1980, it went down to 16.0.

These figures do not mean that the tendency toward higher density in the cities has come to an end. Rather, the large cities have reached a saturation point and their residents are now gravitating toward the surrounding areas, where crowding and land prices are still within tolerable levels and it is possible to commute to work.

Table 4. Changes in the Population of the Six Largest Cities (in ten thousands)

	1950	1955	1960	1965	1970	1975	1980
Tokyo	539	697	831	899	884	864	835
Osaka	196	255	301	316	298	278	265
Nagoya	103	134	159	194	204	208	209
Yokohama	95	114	138	179	224	262	277
Kyoto	110	120	128	137	142	146	147
Kobe	77	98	111	122	129	136	137

This has caused the metropolitan areas to expand in the form of misshapen doughnuts. The populations in the areas around the capital (Tokyo, Kanagawa, Saitama and Chiba), the Chūkyō area (Aichi, Gifu and Mie), and the Kinki area (Osaka, Hyōgo, Kyoto and Nara) are steadily increasing. The population of these three metropolitan areas made up 39.2 percent of the national total in 1960; 45.6 percent in 1970; and in 1980 47.8 percent, which is almost half.

The other aspect of concentration in metropolitan areas is the large flow from rural areas into the urban. This has had the effect of causing overcrowding in the cities and excessive diminution of population in the rural districts. The term "excessive diminution" (*kaso*) first appeared in a 1966 report of the Regional Economy Committee of the Economic Council, at a time when the population concentration in the established industrial regions was becoming a serious problem despite measures for regional dispersion of industry and new industrial cities.

Even between 1955 and 1960 the downtrend in the rural population was already becoming conspicuous, as shown in Table 5. In the 1960–65 period the number of regions with diminishing population decreased, but where it did occur the rate of decline was very great. During the years 1965–70 the rise of urban population slowed down somewhat, and during the 1970–75 and 1975–80 periods there were no regions with diminishing population. This is possibly a result of the dispersion of industry.

If we examine these developments on a local level, we find that in the five years from 1955 to 1960 the populations of 26 prefec-

Table 5. Changes in Population Increases by Region (%)

	Population increase rate					Percentage against nationwide increase				
	1955–1960	1960–1965	1965–1970	1970–1975	1975–1980	1955–1960	1960–1965	1965–1970	1970–1975	1975–1980
All Japan	4.7	5.2	5.5	7.0*	4.6*	100.0	100.0	100.0	100.0*	100.0*
Hokkaido	5.6	2.6	0.2	3.0	4.5	6.4	2.7	0.2	2.1	4.8
Tōhoku	–0.1	–2.3	–0.8	2.2	3.7	–0.2	–4.5	–1.4	2.8	8.2
Northern Kantō	–1.6	0.9	3.8	7.7	6.9	–2.1	0.9	3.7	5.7	5.3
Southern Kantō	15.8	17.6	14.7	12.1	6.1	58.9	64.9	56.9	40.2	24.5
Hokuriku-Tōsan	–1.0	–1.1	–0.3	3.2	3.1	–1.9	–1.8	–0.4	3.4	7.1
Tōkai	6.3	8.3	7.8	8.1	4.6	14.4	17.3	15.7	13.0	11.4
Eastern Kinki	–0.4	3.1	5.8	9.5	7.7	–0.3	1.7	2.9	3.7	2.9
Western Kinki	12.1	14.6	11.2	8.0	2.9	29.7	34.3	27.0	15.9	13.8
Chūgoku	–0.7	–1.1	1.8	5.3	3.0	–1.1	–1.5	2.3	5.1	6.5
Shikoku	–2.9	–3.6	–1.8	3.5	3.0	–3.0	–3.0	–1.3	1.9	3.6
Kyushu	–0.3	–4.1	–2.4	3.4*	4.5*	–0.8	–11.0	–5.5	6.1*	12.0*
Total of Southern Kantō, Western Kinki, and Tōkai	12.2	14.4	12.0	10.0	4.9	103.0	116.5	99.5	69.2	49.7

* Including Okinawa Prefecture

tures declined. In 1960–65 there were 25 such prefectures, but the rate of decline was notably greater. Between 1965 and 1970 only 20 prefectures lost population, and with a few exceptions the rate of decline had also dropped. During the 1970–75 period, population decline occurred in only five prefectures, namely, Akita, Yamagata, Shimane, Saga, and Kagoshima. According to the 1980 census, population increased in all prefectures but one, Tokyo, which had never lost population throughout the postwar period. Thus, although we have seen striking population changes in prefectures in Tōhoku, Chūgoku, Shikoku and Kyushu, at the same time we can note a general increase in their cities. Considering population increase trends in cities by size, we find that from 1960 to 1965 the increase was extremely rapid in cities with populations between 500,000 and 1,000,000, but from 1965 to 1970 the rate of increase for these cities dropped, while cities with populations of 200,000 to 300,000 had the highest rate. The increase in large cities with populations of one million or more was a mere 3 percent. During the 1970–75 and 1975–80 periods, population increases in big cities with populations over 500,000 declined further while the rate of increase in small cities showed a slight increase.

A point to be noted here is that there has been a slight decline in the populations of cities under 30,000 but an increase in that of towns over 30,000. This increase of town populations well reflects the population increases in the major cities. In contrast, towns and villages under 20,000, especially villages under 5,000, have shown an enormous decline which clearly shows the rapid progress of excessive diminution. However, when we compare the changes in the five years from 1970 to 1975 with those for the five years from 1975 to 1980, the decline ratio is quite small. Among the cities, towns and villages nationwide, those which showed decreases during the 1965–70 period were 71 percent; during the 1970–75 period they were 56 percent, and less than half during the 1975–80 period. This can be interpreted as indicating that overcrowding in cities and excessive diminution in the agrarian villages are slowing down in recent years. However, this only indicates that the change has become less rapid than it was during the period of high economic growth; even at present, excessive diminu-

Table 6. Population Increase Rate of Cities, and of Towns and Villages (%)

		1960–65	1965–70	1970–75	1975–80
Cities	Population of one million or more	9.1	3.2	2.5	0.1
	500,000–999,999	24.6	14.1	14.9	6.2
	300,000–499,999	13.9	13.1	13.6	7.4
	200,000–299,999	14.8	17.3	12.6	7.6
	100,000–199,999	16.9	15.0	12.7	7.0
	50,000– 99,999	7.8	10.6	11.9	7.4
	30,000– 49,999	–1.0	0.3	4.7	2.9
	Less than 30,000	–8.6	–8.5	–5.4	–1.8
Towns and villages	More than 30,000	33.3	41.4	37.4	24.1
	20,000– 29,999	0.3	3.2	8.0	8.2
	10,000– 19,999	–4.2	–2.7	1.6	3.4
	5,000– 9,999	–8.3	–8.0	–3.7	–1.1
	Less than 5,000	–13.4	–14.0	–9.2	–5.0
Nationwide		5.2	5.5	7.0	4.6

tion in the remote districts is still going on. During the past five years, 80 percent of the towns and villages under 10,000 and about 10 percent of the villages under 5,000 are showing population decreases.

What is the significance of greater urban concentration and a decline in rural population? The report of the Regional Economy Committee of the Economic Council, reflecting the rise in the 1960–65 concentration of population in the cities, considered this unavoidable and not necessarily unfavorable, provided the cities were not overcrowded. However, excessively large cities are not desirable, while a balanced distribution of population over the nation definitely is.

Can the Japanese archipelago be "remodelled" to achieve this, and can urban pollution be controlled so that it will not become more widespread with "remodelling"? These are serious problems we face in dealing with present trends in population distribution.

3.   Population Structure by Industry

Of those gainfully employed at the time of the Meiji Restoration, 80 percent or more were engaged in agriculture, with a little over 10 percent engaged in commerce and industry. Thereafter, while absolute numbers in the agricultural population did not decrease, population increases went into other industries, with a resulting annual decline in the proportion of the agrarian population. In 1930 it was less than half; in 1940 it sank below 40 percent—even with the addition of those engaged in forestry and fishing it did not exceed 44 percent. Wartime destruction of industry brought this proportion up again, and for a time after the war it exceeded 45 percent. The population in primary industries amounted to 53 percent of the total employed population (see Table 7). But when the economy turned from restoration to growth, the agricultural population dropped below 40 percent, less than before the war, and this proportion continued to fall rapidly year by year. According to the 1980 census, it had fallen to 9.7 percent, and the population in primary industries was slightly under 11 percent.

This precipitous postwar decline in the agricultural population was unprecedented anywhere in the world. Soon after the end of World War II, the influx of wartime evacuees from the cities and repatriates into the rural districts inflated the agricultural population to 18 million, 4 million more than the almost steady 14 million in agriculture from the Meiji Restoration until the end of the war. By 1960 this had shrunk in actual numbers to what it was before the war, and it declined sharply thereafter as the rate of economic growth continued to soar. The 1970 census showed an agricultural population of about 10 million, of which 7 million were engaged full-time in farming; thus in a mere twenty years the number had been reduced to half. In 1980, after another ten years, agrarian population was 5.4 million, of which 4.1 million were engaged full-time in farming.

The shrinkage in numbers in agriculture reduces its relative size in the total employed population. In 1961 the agricultural population had returned to the prewar level, 30 percent of the total. Six or seven years later the proportion was not quite 20 percent, or just below 10 million. A rapid drop of 4 million in the agricultural and an increase of 5 million in the total employed population caused the agricultural population to drop from 30 to 20 percent within a few years, and at present it is below 10 percent. These figures indicate the speed with which Japan's industry has grown; in the short span of twenty-five years beginning in 1955, the proportion of population in primary industries has dropped from 40 to about 10 percent.

The decline in the proportion of population in primary industries was accompanied by a rise in secondary industries to one-third of the total employed population, while the proportion of those employed in tertiary industries rose from about 30 percent to more than half the total. In the course of a soaring economic growth manufacturing grew the most, followed by construction, wholesale and retail trade and services. The present population by industry is shown in Table 7: primary industries, a little over 10 percent; secondary industries, a little over 30 percent; and tertiary industries, a little over 50 percent. In the advanced countries of Europe and America the proportion of those employed

Table 7. Employed Population by Industry (census figures, %)

	1940	1950	1955	1960	1965	1970	1975	1980
Primary industries	44.0	48.5	41.1	32.7	24.7	19.3	13.8	10.9
Agriculture	41.4	45.4	38.0	30.1	22.9	17.9	12.6	9.7
Forestry	0.9	1.2	1.3	1.0	0.5	0.4	0.3	0.3
Fishing	1.7	1.9	1.8	1.5	1.3	1.0	0.9	0.8
Secondary industries	26.1	21.8	23.4	29.1	31.5	34.0	34.1	33.5
Mining	1.8	1.6	1.4	1.2	0.7	0.4	0.2	0.2
Construction	3.0	4.3	4.5	6.1	6.4	7.5	8.9	9.6
Manufacturing	21.3	15.8	17.5	21.7	24.4	26.1	24.9	23.6
Tertiary industries	29.2	29.6	35.5	38.2	43.7	46.6	51.8	55.4
Wholesale & retail trade	12.7	11.1	13.9	15.8	17.8	19.3	21.4	22.7
Finance; insurance	0.9	1.0	1.5	1.6	2.0	2.1	2.6	2.9
Real estate	0.1	0.0	0.1	0.2	0.4	0.5	0.7	0.8
Transportation; communication	4.3	4.4	4.6	5.0	6.0	6.2	6.3	6.2
Electric power; gas; water supply	0.4	0.6	0.6	0.5	0.6	0.6	0.6	0.6
Service industries	9.0	9.2	11.4	12.0	13.8	14.6	16.4	18.6
Public service	1.9	3.3	3.5	3.0	3.1	3.3	3.7	3.6
Not classifiable	0.7	0.1	0.0	0.2	0.1	0.1	0.3	0.2

Table 8. Composition of Employed Population by Employment Status (%)

	1950	1955	1960	1965	1970	1975	1980
Employees	39.5	45.8	54.0	60.9	64.5	69.8	71.9
Self-employed proprietors	26.1	23.9	22.0	19.6	19.3	17.4	17.2
Family workers	34.4	30.0	24.0	19.5	16.2	12.7	10.9

in tertiary industries surpasses that in secondary industries. From Table 7 it can be seen that employment in primary industries in Japan has dropped to where it approaches the pattern of Europe and America; perhaps this is a sign that Japan has become an "advanced" nation.

Such figures alone, however, do not indicate a level of advancement equal to other economically powerful nations. In Japan the number of individual proprietors and family workers is relatively higher than in western Europe or the United States. Most are engaged in agriculture, forestry, fishing or in commerce. In 1955 over half of all the non-employed were from this group. The rapid growth of Japan's economy has greatly changed this population structure. At present the proportion of employed has risen to 70 percent. But even this figure is still far from the 80 to 90 percent reached in some countries. Commerce and the service industries are relatively large; but the number of family enterprises in commerce is still large, most individual proprietors carry on their businesses by themselves, and a great many engage in physical labor and do not differ greatly from manual laborers.

Now let us take a look at the make-up of the manufacturing industry, which has undergone the most remarkable growth. There have been striking changes in its composition by kinds of industry in recent years. Before the war the spinning and weaving industry held an overwhelmingly dominant position, but recently its relative importance has declined sharply. In 1935 manufacturers in the metalworking, machine and chemical industries totaled 36 percent, less than the 41 percent in spinning and weaving, but in 1955 they represented 43 percent of the total, while at present they account for about one-half the total. This points to the fact that the heavy and chemical industries have become increasingly important since the war. And within these industries there has been especially remarkable development in the machine and electrical appliance industries. Before the war these industries employed no more than 15 percent of those engaged in manufacturing, but they now employ 30 percent. They enjoyed a remarkable expansion largely because of increased investments in plants and equipment and in the demand for electrical household appliances and automobiles. In the course of conversion to heavy and chemical industries, especially the machine industry, mammoth corporations which rank among the largest in the world have developed in Japanese industry.

However, as will be seen later, small businesses and midget industries still constitute a considerable proportion. Coupled with the large number of individual proprietors and family workers, the abundance of these small industries is one feature of the dual structure of Japan's economy. In 1968 a survey of the labor force in 1967 was made public; it gave the proportion of the agricultural population as 19.3 percent. In 1968 Japan surpassed West Germany in gross national product and ranked second behind the United States in the free world. Japan was at last becoming accepted as one of the advanced nations. Even though still back in twenty-first place in per capita income, Japan was first in shipbuilding and radio production; second in automobiles, television sets, rayon and synthetic fiber; and third in iron and steel and cotton spinning. There thus was no lack of indices to show that Japan was an advanced nation, and the rapid growth of the economy became the object of world-wide admiration.

This did not mean, however, that industry as a whole had achieved a balanced form of modernization. Extraordinary growth moved Japan from sixth or seventh place in gross national product, where she ranked with Italy, to third place, behind only the United States and the USSR—in only ten years. This growth not only destroyed the environment but also imposed a strain on the development of society, giving rise to many new problems today.

4. Class Structure

There has been considerable change in the class structure of society since the Meiji period, largely because of the development of a capitalist economy and the decline in the status of landlords after the land reform. From the Restoration until about the middle of the Meiji period, the proportion of landlords in the ruling class was high, and since there were few industrial workers, those below, the "ruled," were mostly poor tenant farmers. So in spite of the development of capitalism, the most important class relationship in Japanese society as a whole was that between landlord and tenant. From the last years of Meiji into the Taishō period (1912–26) however, the relative size of the capitalist class increased, as did the number of laborers. The last years of Taishō and the early years of Shōwa (1926–) saw a complete shift from landlord to capitalist as the dominant component of the ruling class, and the landlord thereafter was relegated to the background. Thus, after the war the landlord class disappeared from the class structure.

Immediately after the war, however, independent proprietors still constituted almost 60 percent of the total and the old middle class was still large. Table 9, compiled from censuses, shows that the salaried class, mainly white-collar workers, then amounted to only a little over 10 percent. This class conformation naturally resulted from the fact that the number engaged in agriculture was still large; including family workers, they made up 45 percent of the total.

Changes that followed, however, brought with them steady decreases in the proportion of those engaged in agriculture, forestry and fishing. This was accompanied by a decrease in independent proprietors from 60 percent in 1950 to less than 30 percent in 1970, while the "working class" increased from just under 40 to over 60 percent. Thus, the trend in the latter case was just the reverse of that for independent proprietors. While the salaried class almost doubled, from just over 10 to a little less than 20 percent, productive workers rose from 20 to 30 percent, and those engaged in commercial and service industries and nonproductive workers in general almost tripled.

Today's class structure appears as a handful of capitalists at the top followed by the old middle class of independent proprietors, mainly farmers (a little over 10 percent of the total) and shop owners and service industry workers (less than 10 percent); the new middle class, composed of salaried workers (about 20 percent) and a small number of specialized technicians; and finally the working class (about 40 percent).

The above figures are, however, just a convenient rearrangement of the census results and do not necessarily show the complexity of the real situation. For example, the capitalist class increased from 1.9 percent in 1950 to 2.0 percent in 1955, 2.7 percent in 1960, 3.6 percent in 1965, 5.0 percent in 1970, and 5.9 percent in 1975, but these figures include many individual owners of small-scale businesses who have incorporated for tax purposes and become company officials. Also, members of the old middle class engaged in agriculture, forestry and fishing vary in their

Table 9. Class Structure (%)

	1950	1955	1960	1965	1970	1975
Capitalists	1.9	2.0	2.7	3.6	5.0	5.9
Persons in security services	0.9	1.1	1.1	1.2	1.2	1.4
Self-employed proprietors	58.9	53.2	45.7	38.3	34.8	29.4
Agriculture, forestry & fishing	44.6	37.7	30.6	23.0	18.1	12.7
Mining, manufacturing transportation & communication	6.2	6.2	6.2	6.2	7.3	6.8
Selling	6.2	7.0	6.2	5.9	5.5	5.2
Service workers	0.9	1.5	1.6	1.9	2.3	2.6
Professionals & specialized technicians	1.0	0.9	1.0	1.2	1.6	2.1
Working class	38.2	43.6	50.5	56.9	59.0	63.3
Salaried employees	11.9	12.5	14.2	17.0	18.3	21.3
Productive workers	20.0	22.4	27.8	29.2	29.3	28.2
Nonproductive workers	4.3	6.8	7.8	9.3	10.1	11.5
Unemployed	2.0	1.9	0.7	1.4	1.3	2.3

scale of management; many of them have an auxiliary occupation, doing the same work as laborers.

In practical terms, those who can ally themselves with politicians and high-ranking bureaucrats—the capitalists and top managers of large corporations—have become the ruling class. The roughly 2,210 Japanese corporations capitalized at one billion yen or more constitute no more than 0.2 percent of all enterprises but own 65 percent of the total capital. Moreover, the greater part of industry is virtually controlled by a few giant enterprises. The large number of small enterprises and the high degree of monopoly control are two striking features of Japanese industry. It is those who control the giant enterprises who run Japan.

One de facto result is that the owners of medium, small, and really tiny enterprises fall into the category of the ruled, controlled by those above them. There exist distinct social strata within these groups, however; the owners of medium and small enterprises cannot be lumped together with the mini-owners, nor are they equally "ruled" from above. The former might be called a social stratum of "petty rulers."

Consider also the class of independent proprietors, which, as stated above, has sharply decreased. The scant 7 percent of independent, self-supporting farm families and the farm families with secure auxiliary occupations who are living relatively prosperous lives cannot be lumped together as "farm families" in the same class as those suffering from poverty. Nor can categorical statements be made about urban independent proprietors. Except for a small number who could become a class of petty urban "rulers," most support themselves in insecure businesses, using the labor of their own families. Unlike the farm families, their group includes a considerably unstable stratum in which frequent bankruptcies occur. This stratum is constantly threatened by failure, setting it distinctly apart from the few who have established themselves in relative security as a single, uniform class of independent urban proprietors.

Likewise, the upper and lower strata of the working class cannot simply be lumped together as "workers." The difference between the new middle class of white-collar workers and the so-called laboring blue-collar class has been decreasing as the status of the former declines and the wages of the latter rise, but there still is a gap between them. Even within the blue-collar group, the wage levels of those in large corporations and those working for medium and small ones have been drawing closer together, but the two are still regarded as different groups.

The higher productivity of labor appears to be causing a slowdown in the relative increase of productive workers. This trend will probably produce a net decrease in the future. Nonproductive workers engaged in selling and services, however, are rapidly rising in numbers. They may be "workers," but they cannot be considered in the same category with productive labor. A third group is public service workers; they also comprise a relatively large group but they, too, cannot be identified with the other two.

The least favored class are workers in tiny enterprises, unemployed workers, and middle-aged and elderly people who are reentering employment. They compose the lowest strata of society. They include 2.4 percent of all households (still 12 persons out of 1,000) that are either on welfare for their livelihood or in a borderline stratum of those who may at any time fall into the category of those "on welfare." People in these classes, who are at the very bottom of the "ruled" classes, are the greatest losers in Japan's economic growth.

What is the relationship of the class structure we have described to the realities of Japanese society? Although the following pages are too short to analyze that relationship in each case, it forms the underlying theme of this brief description. It is this relationship that must be considered, both by observers and participants, in any attempt to understand the weaknesses or strengths of Japanese society.

II. The Family and Socialization

1. Changes in the Family Structure

From the Tokugawa period until the end of World War II the Japanese family system was governed by the concept of *ie* (house or family)*, which followed the samurai ideal and was legally recognized even in the Meiji civil code. The *ie* was inherited by the oldest son, who continued to live after marriage in the same house with his father, the head of the *ie*, and his mother. Children whose jobs took them away from their birthplaces had to live apart from their ancestral homes, but most oldest sons stayed home, so that there were often two or three generations living in the same household. When a younger son left the *ie* and established his own "branch" household, it became a nuclear family in form but was still bound through lineage to the main family he had left, and would eventually become another extended family.

The average household had about five members. This number was expected to decrease after the postwar revision of the civil code, which attempted to establish a legal basis for the nuclear family as a norm. Actually, it temporarily increased slightly, and there was no decrease in average family size throughout the period of economic recovery. Most observers agree that the postwar baby boom and a severe housing shortage that did not permit the breakup of families were prime factors in the increase. A decrease only began with the transition from recovery to growth. In 1955 the average household was 4.97 members, about the same as before the war. In 1960 it had decreased to 4.54, and by 1965, to 4.05. According to the 1970 census, it had dropped below 4—to 3.69; in the 1975 census, it had dropped to 3.44, and in 1980 it

---

* *Ie* means "house," both in the ordinary sense and in the more abstract meaning of "family," as in the context of "family lineage, family tradition," etc.

31

was 3.33. Projections by the Population Research Institute indicate that this trend will continue, and by 1985 it will have decreased to 3.17.

An average of three persons per household is comparable to levels now prevailing in parts of Europe and the United States, and in addition, the sharp increase in the number of households is directly related to the increase in recent years of nuclear families. A decline in the size of farm families, where the extended family system still survives, has resulted from fewer children born to such families and younger sons leaving the family (*ie*) early. But in city households the recent trend for the oldest son, as well, to set up a household apart from his parents after he marries is the main cause of a decrease in the size of urban families.

Table 10 shows the distribution of households by number of members; it clearly shows the decrease in family size. For example, in 1930 about 60 percent of all families had five members or less, and at the present time more than 90 percent fall in this category. While the decline in the birth rate has been an important reason for the greater number of small families than before the war, the fact that single-member households have doubled and nuclear families have increased must be taken into account.

Looking at types of family structure, we notice there are fewer families with three generations living together and more with only

Table 10. Percentages of Households by Number of Members

Number	1930	1955	1960	1965	1970	1975	1980
1	5.5	3.5	5.2	8.1	10.8	13.7	15.8
2	11.7	10.8	12.7	14.3	15.4	16.9	17.6
3	14.8	14.5	15.9	18.2	19.7	20.1	19.0
4	15.1	16.6	18.7	22.3	25.5	26.5	26.6
5	14.5	16.7	17.1	16.2	14.5	12.4	11.6
6	12.7	14.1	13.1	10.6	8.4	6.4	6.0
7	9.9	10.3	8.5	6.1	3.5	2.8	2.5
8	6.8	6.5	4.6	2.5	1.4	0.9	0.7
9 or more	9.0	7.1	4.2	1.8	0.8	0.4	0.2
Average	4.98	4.97	4.54	4.05	3.69	3.44	3.33

Table 11. Households by Type of Family Structure (%)

	1955	1960	1965	1970	1975	1980
Kinship households	96.1	94.9	91.8	88.8	86.2	84.0
1. Nuclear family households	59.6	60.2	62.6	63.4	64.0	63.4
Husband & wife only	6.8	8.3	9.9	10.9	12.5	13.1
Husband, wife & children	43.1	43.4	45.4	46.0	45.7	44.3
Father & children	1.6	1.3	1.0	1.0	0.8	0.9
Mother & children	8.1	7.3	6.3	5.5	4.0	5.1
2. Other kinship households	36.5	34.7	29.2	25.5	22.2	20.7
Nonkinship households	0.5	0.4	0.4	0.4	0.2	0.2
Single-member households	3.4	4.7	7.8	10.8	13.7	15.8

one generation. More striking is the increase in the number of nuclear families composed of one married couple and their children, or families with only husband and wife. If to these families we add those consisting only of father and children or mother and children and call them nuclear families, then the number of such families amounted to slightly less than 60 percent of the total according to the 1955 census, but it stood at 63 percent in 1980. From Table 11 one can also see that families with only husband and wife doubled and there has been a significant decline in the proportion of "other kinship households," which consist mainly of three-generation households.

Although nuclear families exceed 60 percent, we cannot say that all of them are genuinely "nuclear" (composed only of a married couple and their unmarried children). Many are only transitionally nuclear families and will eventually become direct lineage families with the married children living under the same roof.

Nevertheless, the decrease in members per household and the simplified relationships in families are symptoms that the whole family structure has been undergoing considerable change in recent years; the change is expressed by the term "nuclear family" or kaku kazoku (meaning "change to the nuclear family") in Japanese. "Nuclear family" came into general use as a sociological term after G.P. Murdock's publication *Social Structure* in 1949. But

until twenty years ago there was no established Japanese translation for this term, even in the field of sociology. Today it has
become part of our general vocabulary, thus attesting to the rapid
rate of change in the Japanese family structure.

2.   The Dissolution of the *Ie* and Its Survival

Before the war Japanese ranked their firmly established institution of *ie* along with their unique "national polity" as superior
traits which they could flaunt before other countries and cultures.
The family was simply a concrete manifestation of the *ie*, a legal
reality, a concept and a physical entity handed down as inheritance in direct succession from generation to generation. The head-
ship was inherited by the oldest son, and he also succeeded to the
family estate. His wife became a member of her husband's *ie* and
was considered, literally, "a woman of the *ie*," as is implied by the
Japanese character for "bride" (*yome*)—"woman" plus "house."
Members of a family were trained to suppress individual desires
and make the goal of their lives the maintenance of the *ie* and the
enhancement of its name. While this was not always true for every
class of society, for most Japanese families the *ie*-oriented life was
commonly accepted.

The revision of the civil code after the war reflected a rejection
of the legal dominance of the *ie* over the individual. Article 24 of
the Constitution expressly provides for the dignity of the individual
and the equality of the sexes in family life. Marriage was stipulated
to rest on the mutual consent of the two parties involved. This
meant new principles of the modern family in the foundations of
the civil code. The era when a new wife's name was added to the
family register of the head of the house came to an end. The very
term "head of the family," was abolished, and when a marriage
is registered, a new husband-and-wife family register is set up. As
a matter of law, this meant the rejection of the old direct-lineage
family system and the adoption of the one-married-couple system
based on the nuclear family. As a result, inheritance of the head-
ship of the *ie* is no longer possible; inheritance itself has become

limited to the estate of the deceased. Along with establishment of the wife's rights to such an inheritance, there was provision for an equal division of the estate among children, regardless of their sex.

These new laws symbolized a revolution in Japanese family life. The revised civil code was a challenge to the ages-old *ie* system peculiar to Japan and to the old traditions behind it.

The challenge did not bring about the immediate breakup of the system. A revolution in legislation could not bring about a revolution in practice, and the *ie* system still survives in custom. But change in the official attitudes toward the family was bound to have an effect on actual life. There was a short period when people once again called for revival of the *ie* system, but on the whole there has been almost no resistance to the modernization of family life, even during the period of reaction which followed the early postwar wave of democratization. Although the direct-lineage *ie* system survives as a custom, it is gradually disintegrating.

A factor that seems to have been important in the disintegration of the *ie* is a decline in "*ie*-consciousness." A sense of family status was especially tenacious in the relatively fixed, unchanging society of the rural areas, but in the cities it had begun to lose its grip even before the war. Consciousness of family status certainly did not disappear in the cities, but in urban society, as one's economic position rises, one's family status also can easily rise. In modern Japan consciousness of status hierarchy strongly persisted while the barriers between classes became increasingly weak, and a rise in economic level was directly connected with a rise in family status and social position. This situation brought about an intensive race to get ahead in the world. The consciousness of family status, however, grew much weaker in the cities after the war. Even in rural areas family consciousness was diminishing, as the effects of new laws and changes in family status that resulted from the land reform were slowly absorbed. One full generation has matured since the breakup of the landlord system in the immediate postwar period. Now, the hierarchical status relationship between families based on the landlord-tenant tie is increasingly thought of as a tale of the distant past. Despite their strong sense of family property, most farm families now regard farmland and mountain forest simply as the most dependable kind of property;

this is a different attitude from that of an earlier era, when they were regarded as symbols of family status.

This diminishing family consciousness carries with it a decline in the authority of the head of the *ie*, who before had been both its representative and the leader of the family members. Today, after one generation, the term "head of the family" has disappeared and Japanese families in general are no longer the authoritarian little autocracies that they once were. The transition from "head of the family" (*koshu*) to "head of the household" (*setainushi*) is bound up with the breakdown in the dominant positions of the patriarchal head, the father and male children. In the transition from the parent-and-child oriented family, in which male children were given priority, to the husband-and-wife oriented family with equality of the sexes as a basic premise, the general position of females has risen. There is some truth in the expression, "Since the war nylon stockings and women have grown stronger." Women have by no means attained a position equal to that of men, but within the family the position of women has become incomparably stronger than before the war. Marriage, too, has changed. Before the war marriage was usually for the sake of the *ie* and the woman became more a daughter-in-law of the *ie* than the wife of her husband. The mere fact that now mutual consent of the two parties is considered important represents a great change. In general the will of the parents was the important thing before the war, but today consideration is given first to the wishes of the persons contracting the marriage. Even now, except in the large cities, it seems marriages by *omiai* (arranged meeting between a man and a woman with a view to marriage) predominate over those resulting from "love" matches, but it has become common for these meetings to be supplemented by "dating." What a vast change from before the war, when it was common for a couple to talk at length to each other only after they were married! The honeymoon, also, has changed from the preserve of only a few to become a general custom even in the rural districts—something unthinkable thirty years ago.

The average age at which women first marry has recently risen to 25 and over, as opposed to an average of 23 during the first years of Shōwa (which began in 1926). This is probably because the percentage of females pursuing higher education has risen—they now slightly exceed the number of males in high school and are gaining on male enrollment in college—and because the proportion of those employed has increased. The age of marriage for men dropped temporarily after the war, but at present is about 28—not very different from what it was in the early years of Shōwa. Where once there was a difference of four years or more in the ages of husbands and wives, it now is only 2.5 years. If more and better housing were available and income levels were improved, the age of marriage, now relatively high compared with other countries, would probably drop somewhat and the difference in age between husband and wife would probably decrease. In any case, the smaller difference in ages between spouses compared with prewar figures is also related to changes in the whole view of marriage and of husband-wife relations.

It is considered preferable for a newly married couple in the cities to live apart from their parents. An upper-class family, even if it has room in the same house for the new couple, may have a new house built instead. Or, because of the high price of land, it is fairly common for the parents to build a new house on their own lot for the couple. Middle-and lower-class newlyweds commonly do not have the funds to assure their independence, and they often live apart from their parents in rented rooms, with parental assistance. Such changes have spurred on the trend toward making the nuclear family the norm.

In Japan as a whole, however, the tendency to establish a new home upon marriage is not yet a completely established way of life. In the rural districts it is still considered normal for the new couple to live in the same house with the husband's parents, and among urban independent proprietors the eldest son and his wife are, if possible, housed in the same dwelling with his parents. The movement in the cities toward the nuclear family, furthermore, is fostered by a chronic housing shortage, which persists today even though the bad conditions following the war have been ameliorated. Nevertheless, the average house almost never has enough space for two generations to live together.

Legally, the system of inheritance has changed to provide for equal division of the estate among the children, but estates are not actually being divided. Primarily because of the wishes of the parents, estates are still being divided with preference given to the family "successor"; such a division is accompanied by a promise from the heir to take care of them in their old age. This way of dealing with property and parents is very widespread among farm families and among the urban old middle class also. It is also apparent among relatively upper-class urban groups. Even though the oldest son lives independently, his parents usually think of him, rather than of a younger son or a daughter, when they contemplate how to handle the difficulties they will face in their old age. For that reason the greater share of their property is expected to go to the oldest son.

The prewar *ie* system has, then, been broken up, but to a great extent the tradition survives as custom. It will probably grow weaker, but the rate of disintegration will depend on whether or not public social security programs and individual savings can provide security for the aged. The trend toward the nuclear family is probably irreversible and will grow, but the problem of what to do about the aged will become more serious. Life expectancy is now 73.5 years for males and 78.9 for females; old age is no longer the brief period it was before the war, when the average life expectancy was under 50. If security for the aged were guaranteed, the movement toward the nuclear family would accelerate, probably becoming a welcome symbol of happy family life. But in Japan this road is still narrow and the problem of the aged is serious. The breakup of the *ie* and long delay in the provision of security for old age leaves a gap which, with the swing to the nuclear family, will probably become wider. Meanwhile, for lack of another alternative the *ie* system survives in a distorted form.

3.   The Nuclear Family: Its Assets and Drawbacks

The modern Japanese family is going through a transition from the old direct-lineage family to the new one-married-couple family. While moving toward liberation from the binding strictures of the past, the family as an institution is also losing the security for the aged that it once provided. According to surveys by the Ministry of Health and Welfare, more than 60 percent of those 65 years of age or older were living with their children in 1980, although the percentage itself had been decreasing gradually. However, the percentage of those 65 years of age or older who are supported by their families has dropped considerably in a short period of time: from 77 percent in 1957 to 65 percent in 1963, and to 56 percent in 1968. Furthermore, as shown in Table 12, a public opinion survey by the Prime Minister's Office about the life and the problems of the aged revealed that the proportion of those who consider security for the aged to be the responsibility of the family was 34 percent in 1969, but it declined to 22 percent in 1973. On the contrary, those who consider that the responsibility should be taken on by the nation or society increased during those years from 15 percent to 24 percent. The public opinion survey also showed that the opinion that the aged should be cared for by themselves or society became more widely held as the age of the respondents fell. For example, of those from 20 to 29 years old, only 16 percent considered the elderly to be a family responsibility. Today, when one cannot buy a home with retirement pay and when social security has only a brief history and its level is low, the picture of family life is far brighter than before the war but is still shadowed by dark anxiety about old age.

In this transition period it is the urban working class which has most rapidly promoted the change to the nuclear family. Many in this class are housed in concrete apartment developments that have gradually been becoming more numerous even though they provide only cramped living quarters. The "2 DK" unit (two

Table 12. Changes in Opinions about Who Should Support the Aged (%)

| | Total | | Respondents over 60 | |
	1969	1973	1969	1973
The aged person himself	33	29	29	25
Children or family	34	22	39	27
Nation or society	15	24	12	21
DK, cannot generalize	18	25	20	27

rooms and a dinette-kitchen), so far regarded as standard, is equipped with electrical appliances. Twenty years ago "development" residents aspired to the "three sacred treasures" of refrigerator, washing machine and vacuum cleaner. A couple of years ago the goals became the "three C's"—car, "cooler" (air conditioner) and color television. To achieve these goals both husband and wife often decide to work. According to a 1975 survey on the labor force, almost half (47 percent) of female full-time workers employed in nonagricultural or nonforestry occupations are married. And about one-fourth of unemployed women would like employment; 40 percent or more of them said: "It's not that we are having a difficult time making a living; I just want to earn money for household expenses."

The demand for day-care centers is increasing. Creating more such centers is, in itself, a positive social trend, but both husband and wife continue to work either to raise their standard of living or to get out of public housing and into a home of their own. This may result in an unwilling limitation of the number of children, however, and in the problem of children having to come home to an empty house ("key children," who carry a key to the house or apartment). These developments are not quite happy results of a higher proportion of working women.

Today's housewife has so many electrical appliances that she has too much spare time on her hands. For the more than half who are unemployed, this creates loneliness and isolation. If mothers do not turn their attention to some activity outside the home, the result often is the "education mama" (*kyōiku mama*) who puts all her energy into driving her children to achieve success in school.

Before the war mothers had many children, and by the time their own children were independent they would have grandchildren, born to their oldest sons. Moreover, according to an NHK (National Broadcasting Corporation) survey in 1941, housework required an average of ten and one-half hours a day. The same kind of survey in 1965 revealed that this time had decreased by three and one-half hours. Nearly no difference was found in the results of the 1975 survey, which showed that this average was 7 hours and 40 minutes. At present the national average of babies born per married woman is 1.9, or 1.7 less than it was thirty years ago. There is, then, no comparison between the present and 1930, when this average was 4.7. After a woman is a little past the age of thirty, her children no longer take most of her time. They are sent off to school, and she has only a small apartment to clean, leaving her with nothing to do. This is what creates the loneliness and isolation of the housewife, and it is perhaps boredom that turns her into an "education mama." If only to enable them to escape from this situation, the way should be open for these housewives to re-enter employment after they are free from child care.

These "education mamas," in homes where family-centered "my-home-ism" prevails, may have unsatisfied aspirations but they are at least secure. There are still many families, lower in the social scale, where there is no question about the wife's going back to work; she *has* to work, at home or at a poorly paid part-time job, to supplement her husband's income. In these families there is no choice but to leave the children unattended. The wife has to help earn money for them to *maintain* their standard of living, even if it means leaving the children to fend for themselves. The phenomena of "key children" who come home to wait for their parents has arisen in the salaried class because the father and mother are both working to *raise* their standard of living. The two kinds of families are different in nature, but since neither has grandparents to care for the children they both remain "nuclear" families.

In such households of nuclear families there is no psychological pressure resulting from two generations of married couples living under the same roof. To this extent, they are happier. However, when one takes into account their future prospects, they certainly cannot be as secure as they appear at first glance. This is because the members of such families, in most cases, cannot guarantee a livelihood in old age. And though "home" is called *katei* (*ka*, "house," and *tei*, "yard"), a concrete building without a yard for the children creates problems in raising them. Even if a child does not become autistic as a result of being raised in isolation from others, there is some danger that it will be harmed emotionally. In nuclear families young mothers are freed from interference by mothers-in-law, but they lose the benefit of learning from the experience of the older generation. The era when divorces were caused by the mother-in-law is past, but the danger of permanent rifts between husband and wife is increasing. Until about the middle of the Meiji era Japan's divorce rate was unusually high among the civilized countries: from 2.5 to 3.0 cases per thousand; but it gradually declined thereafter. Although it increased after the war to slightly over 1.0, for the ten years preceding 1965 it remained stationary at about 0.7. It has recently risen again; it was approaching 1.1 in 1975, and in 1980 it was over 1.2. It is easy for psychological estrangement to develop between a husband who expects to find solace and escape from the frustrations of his job in the emotional security of his own home, only to find there a wife whose isolation has turned her into an "education mama," or who is herself tired from work.

The situation is slightly different in farm families where two generations live in the same house and do not face these problems. Life in these families is still more secure than in nuclear families. But the precarious future of agriculture is only one factor that makes this security slightly tenuous.

Most farm families, in an effort to catch up with the rise in the standard of living, have auxiliary occupations. In areas where it is not possible to commute to such jobs, some member or members of the family must live away from home for long periods at a time. Extended absences by the father often leave families without their oldest male member, to be supported by an "absentee" provider. This can sometimes lead to the breakup of the family. And when the mother also must leave the home to do part-time work, the problem of "key children" likewise appears in the rural areas. Shouldering a double load of low-paid day labor and work on the farm in the morning and evening, the mother is often seriously overworked.

Other families even less well off have still more difficulty making a living. They not only receive a meager income but also have less hope than before the war of receiving asistance from relatives. These are households composed of old people or a mother and children. In survey standards set by the Ministry of Health and Welfare, households composed of men 65 years or older and women 60 and older, or elderly people of the latter age level living with children under 18, are considered "aged" households. In 1960 these comprised 2.2 percent of all households; in 1970 this proportion rose to 4.0 percent, and in 1979, 6.5 percent. One-sixth of such households are receiving subsistence allowances from the State. This is eight times the average for households in general, and families of this kind constitute more than one-third of all those receiving public subsistence allowances. Moreover, households consisting of mother and children have increased to more than 1 percent of all households. If we add families with disabled or ill members to the mother-and-children and advanced-age categories, the total by now amounts to about 90 percent of all households receiving public subsistence allowances.

For these families, left behind as the trend toward nuclear families rises, the future is dark, and there is clearly a far greater need now for society to lend a hand than during the era when the *ie* dominated the family system.

4.   Socialization Process and the Generation Gap

The family is very important in the socialization of children. A child learns to talk, is inculcated with the basic patterns of conduct necessary in social life, and forms his early habits in the family into which he is born. Especially until he begins to associate with other children of the neighborhood in a play group, the family is the whole universe for the very young child, and until he enters kindergarten or primary school most of his time is spent with his family. The character formed in this period becomes the basis of his personality. Traces of it will remain in him for the rest of his life, as is indicated in the saying: "What a child is at three he will be at a hundred."

If this is true, then the changes in the Japanese family from the end of the war to the present must have had a great effect on character formation. Deep differences in character have arisen between the generation whose childhoood was spent in prewar families and that which grew up since the war. It is not enough, however, simply to divide people roughly into prewar and postwar generations. There are really three groups now: those raised before the war by the prewar generation; those raised since the war by a generation whose character was formed before the war; and those who have been reared by a generation themselves raised since the war. Though the differences among all of these should be examined, let us here compare socialization in the prewar and the postwar families.

Before the war most Japanese were raised in the extended family. The *ie* was the basis of this upbringing, and in actual practice most children were brought up under the guidance of often pampering grandmothers rather than of their mothers, who had no real authority to discipline them. For a mother, having a child of her own was a condition for gaining security in her husband's family; it also meant rising from a very weak position to one in which she had at least her own child to scold. By scolding her child she could also give vent to her frustrations. More important, perhaps, a child provided an outlet for her affections, for she entered into marriage without knowing her husband very well and with no time to develop a strong affection for him; her love had to be focused on the child. It is from this aspect of the established way of life that we can understand the extraordinarily strong attachment between the Japanese mother and her children.

These children in traditional families received from their mother and grandmother the discipline that resulted in what Ruth Benedict calls "shame culture." They absorbed the deep sensitivity of the older women to outside opinion and the approval or disapproval of those around them, and the child could be sanctioned on the basis of such standards. The father and head of the *ie* operated in the context of this discipline of the mother and grandmother. The discipline stressed conduct that would not cause disgrace, shame or ridicule, rather than what was right or wrong. The child was pampered during childhood, but after a certain age his discipline quickly became rigid, and it was based on what "others" approved of or considered appropriate to society. He was made to understand that the way to get along in the world was to bow to the authority of the head of the *ie* and of influential persons of the neighborhood, and to conform to the patterns of behavior of those around him. This kind of family training was strongly supported by the close-knit communities of the towns and villages, and school education did nothing to weaken it.

Thus the Japanese individual was molded to accept authoritarianism and to cultivate little individual autonomy; the seedbed for his character was the family. With the changing nature of the family after the war, how has this process of socialization changed?

We cannot treat this vast subject in detail, but one of the most conspicuous points in the nuclear family today is that the dual authority in discipline that characterized the direct-lineage family has come to an end. The occasions on which a grandparent might nullify the effect of a reprimand by the mother, for example, no longer arise. Nor is the authority of the head of the *ie* any longer necessary to back up family discipline as a generally accepted practice. Parents, however, have been unable to break away from pampering the child in early childhood, as they themselves were pampered. They cannot shift to democratic or autonomous discipline that will make the child capable of independent self-control as he grows older. Parents of the prewar generation, in particular, have had their confidence in the values by which they were raised shaken since the war; not knowing how to construct a new set of values, they were not sure how to bring up their children. Children who were raised in this confusion are now trying to bring up their own children. This young generation of parents, impelled to bring up their children differently from the way they were treated, have not yet established a method of socializing children suitable to the nuclear family.

In the present nuclear family conflict between new and old generations over the training of children no longer arises, but communication among members of the nuclear family is poorer than in the direct-lineage family, particularly because there are fewer people in the household. Socialization in the prewar family, while it produced little personal autonomy, did enjoy a stable direction that the modern nuclear family has failed to find. Today's parents lack self-confidence in childrearing, and they seem to be growing even less certain about what methods are best. In a 1966 public opinion survey by the Prime Minister's Office, respondents were asked to choose the statment that best represented their opinion: "Recent methods are better," or "Those of a generation ago were better." Opinion was almost equally divided between the two. But in a 1971 survey 40 percent of those respondents who were mothers said, "It was better in the old days," as opposed to the 20 percent who said, "It is being done better nowadays." Especially in Tokyo, where mothers in nuclear families are probably more numerous, more than half thought that the old methods were better. This is only one indication that many think their own methods of socialization are inadequate compared with the ways they were brought up. The questionnaire also revealed a high rate of uncertainty about the best child training. In a society in which one's academic career is so important, mothers who lack self-confidence become "education mamas." These women desire only the happiness of their children, yet they do not have the kind of firm conviction that prewar parents had in the value of getting their children into a prestigious school, building the family name or trying to give more to their children than they themselves had. Children today either react against this pressure or they scorn themselves and become egoistic individuals. Some become completely apathetic and conform to their parents' wishes. Except for blind conformism, either of the other two attitudes tends to alienate them from their parents' generation. Only the future can tell whether the kind of family that will mold a new type of Japanese individual will emerge from the "generation gap."

In families which retain the extended or direct-lineage form, socialization is even more complex. The generation of grandparents can no longer maintain their prerogatives in child training that they had before the war, and the younger generation of parents has no set of principles to replace those of their own parents. Loss of self-confidence on the part of parents probably results in individuals quite different from the past, but it will take time for new patterns of socialization and character formation to develop.

The present-day Japanese family has not yet created a basis on which to mold the character of a new Japanese individual. The environment of the nuclear family is producing a great many individuals who are motivated by "my-home-ism" and the pursuit of profit. But some of their children are rebelling against the attitudes that result in such training. This rebellion is producing "hippies" on the one hand, and anti-establishment, anti-war ideologues on the other. This rebellion may turn into something constructive and positive—when more young people grow up with the attitude that the family is more than a place to escape to from society—when they see it as a part of society, a place from which to pursue happiness in society. It seems that a sound and stable direction for Japanese society will emerge when the nuclear family can establish a firm place in the whole society and build patterns of socialization that encourage positive participation outside the home as well as individual happiness inside oneself and one's family.

III. Changes in Rural Society

1. Changing Structure of Agriculture

Japanese agriculture before the war was rooted in a system in which most farming units were extremely small and worked by hand. Half of all cultivated land was controlled by landlords whose tenants did the actual farming. These two factors have been crucial in the agricultural system and also in the far-reaching changes that have occurred since the war.

Japan has been an agricultural country since ancient times, and there has been little possibility of increasing the geographically limited area of cultivated land. The number of farm families, however, who tilled the land remained at an almost constant 5.5 million households from the Meiji Restoration to World War II, despite population growth. Capitalism in Japan grew rapidly, but it drew for its labor force upon only the younger sons of farm families, without stimulating entire families to leave agriculture. Consequently, as Table 13 shows, almost 70 percent of farm families were farming one hectare or less, and over one-third of them had 0.5 hectare or less; this was equivalent to poverty.

From the Meiji period onward tenant farming actually increased. A little over 40 percent of farm families were part-owner, part-tenant farmers; almost 30 percent were entirely tenant farmers. Owner-farmers never amounted to over one-third, thus leaving 70 percent as tenants who had to pay high fees and who bore the added insecurity of impermanent rights of tenancy. Finally, they were forced to subordinate themselves to their landlords.

Because of poverty most farmers were unable to increase productivity through mechanization; instead they lived by the sweat of their labor, striving constantly to enhance productivity per unit area through plant breed improvement and increased use of fer-

Table 13. Distribution of Farm Families by Size of Area Cultivated (%)

	−0.5ha	−1.0	−2.0	−3.0	−5.0	5.0−
1910	37.6	33.0	19.3	5.9	2.9	1.3
1920	35.3	33.3	20.7	6.1	2.8	1.6
1930	34.3	34.3	22.1	5.7	2.3	1.3
1940	33.4	32.8	24.5	5.7	2.2	1.4
1950	40.8	31.9	21.7	3.4	1.3	0.8
1960	38.3	31.7	23.6	3.8	1.5	1.0
1970	37.9	30.2	24.1	4.8	1.7	1.3
1980	41.6	28.2	21.2	5.3	2.2	1.5

tilizer. In the lower classes in urban society there were groups even poorer, but it was the farmer who bore the image of the down-trodden, one who could never escape from poverty no matter how hard he worked. Agriculture served as the vital stepping stone to the development of capitalism, but it was left behind, never to benefit from the growth of a capitalist economy.

The postwar land reform freed agriculture from the second characteristic—the domination of tenant farming. With the development of a capitalist economy the influence of the landlord class in Japan began to decline, and from the Taishō period (1912–26) into the early years of Shōwa (1926–) it was replaced entirely by the newly dominant capitalist class. That is why, when production of foodstuffs and cheap rice was considered necessary for restoration of the economy after the war, the Japanese government conceived the idea of land reform. The American Occupation spent a relatively large proportion of its time and energy in preparing even more thorough measures for a total reform of landholding rights and units of land, ultimately breaking up the landlord system and its ancient dominance over rural communities. Most farmers became owners of the land they cultivated.

After the land reform, agriculture saw higher productivity in rice, the main crop; fruit and livestock production also registered remarkable increases. Machinery, which had been used by a few in the early years of Shōwa, was first used for tilling after the war, when small models of cultivators were introduced; recently farm tractors have come into common use as well. At the present time

Japan leads the world in mechanized power used per unit area. Mechanized agriculture also means excessive capital investment for the farm family. The rise in cost of production due to increased expenditures for the purchase of machines and agricultural chemicals has kept farm income low in spite of higher yields.

Until recent years agricultural production rose steadily, but that increase never went beyond 3 or 4 percent annually. In contrast, the gross national product continued to rise at an annual rate of 10 percent or more all through the sixties. While the total economy was soaring, agriculture actually dropped. In 1955 it accounted for almost 20 percent of the national income, but during the era of economic growth it fell below 10 percent and is now only around 3.5 percent. This productivity gap between agriculture and other industries has been steadily widening.

Thus, farm families have become unable to live by agriculture alone, and this has resulted in the drain of farm population away from agriculture. The 1950 farm population of 18 million, or 6.2 million households, fell to about 13.9 million in 1960, and according to a labor force survey in 1980, it had dropped to 5.3 million, way below the result of the census; this means it dropped by two-thirds during these twenty-five years. Its proportion in the overall employed population also dropped in this twenty-year period from 30 to 10 percent.

In spite of the sharp decrease in farm population, however, the number of farm households dropped below 5 million only recently, about 800,000 less than the prewar level of 5.5 million. This is because farming is now carried on mainly by the aged and by women, while large numbers of the young adult male population have left agriculture. The spread of power cultivators has helped to compensate somewhat for the decrease in the farm labor force. For these and other reasons, the number of farm families engaging in other occupations is steadily and rapidly increasing. In 1950, when the economy had not yet recovered from the war, opportunities for employment were scarce and about half of all farm families were engaged exclusively in agriculture. But, as can be seen from Table 14, five years later this proportion had decreased to 35 percent, ten years later to 21 percent, and finally, in 1980, to 13 percent. During the same period the proportion of farm families whose primary source of income was nonagricultural (Type 2 part-time agricultural households) gradually increased from 20-odd percent to 65 percent, where it stands at the present time. Also, at present three-fourths of Japanese farm families have no male member exclusively engaged in agriculture, a telling symbol of the situation of agriculture in Japan today.

Table 14. Percentages of Full-time and Part-time Farm Households

	1941	1950	1955	1960	1965	1970	1975	1980
Full-time	41.5	50.0	34.8	34.3	21.5	15.6	12.4	13.4
Part-time (Type 1)	37.3	28.4	37.7	33.6	36.7	33.7	25.4	21.5
Part-time (Type 2)	21.2	21.6	27.5	32.1	41.8	50.7	62.2	65.1

In 1961 the government undertook a basic reform of the structure of agriculture, beginning with the Basic Law on Agriculture (Nōgyō Kihonhō).

This law, however, did not affect the fundamental structure of agriculture, and it did not suffice to pull agriculture as an economic sector out of the precarious situation into which it had fallen. Waste, inefficiency and above all a self-destructive system were becoming more of a threat every year. Seeking an easy way to change the structure with only a small expenditure of funds, the government annually raised the price of rice in a makeshift effort to achieve some sort of balance. But government purchases of rice from farm families resulted in a rice surplus, which eventually had to reach a limit. In 1969, therefore, the price of rice was left unchanged, and planted acreage was reduced to curtail production. This truly marked a turning point for agriculture in Japan, a country known from ancient times as the "land of abundant rice" (*mizuho no kuni*) and a country where paddy cultivation formed the core of agriculture. For farmers, for whom increased production under the stable food rationing system had constituted the basic support, this brought on a serious crisis.

A rice surplus meant a conversion from rice culture to other crops, but further expansion of livestock-raising or fruit is always accompanied by anxiety. Even if farmers switched to new kinds of products, increasing external pressure on Japan to liberalize imports raises the frightening possibility that Japan may have to compete with foreign agricultural products, a task of which it is incapable at present.

The only course open now is the rationalizing of agriculture and the creation of a class of farmer who can catch up with the rise in the standard of living. At the present time, however, far less than 10 percent of Japanese farmers are able to earn from farming alone an income equal to that of wage and salary earners so as to become "independent" or self-supporting. Further growth in the national income will, in all likelihood, only mean a smaller proportion of independent, self-supporting farm families. Thus it is necessary to begin all over again with structural reform of agriculture in the true sense of the term.

As a by-product of the rapid changes in Japanese agriculture, the nation's self-sufficiency rate for food has become very low; it is a matter of urgent necessity to support existing genuine farm families and increase the size of their farms. If the current situation is allowed to continue, all farm families will of necessity become part-timers. Agriculture cannot be saved unless some measures are taken to enable large numbers to leave the farms and to develop a system which will promote some form of cooperation among those families that remain in agriculture. It has been said that, given the current level of productivity, only one-twentieth of the present farm population would be sufficient to maintain Japan's agriculture. Though it may not be necessary to go to such an extreme, a radical structural reform of agriculture is necessary to resolve the present problem. It must include a long-range, heavy capital investment in social overhead directed toward agriculture, and it must be carried out so that farmers can transfer to other occupations without being put out of work. Conservative party politics, however, are too closely linked with big business for this to be possible. The present conservative government, though criticized for being pro-agrarian, is actually anti-agrarian in the economic and welfare policies it supports.

2. Changing Aspects of Farm Life

It has long been a fixed idea that life in the farm villages is one of poverty and that agricultural society is feudal and rigid. Before the war, certainly, farmers were often living in poverty. According to a report of the 1926–27 survey of family budgets carried out by the Cabinet Bureau of Statistics, the income of the farmer was 70 percent that of the white-collar worker, and 95 percent that of the laborer (whose wages were low enough to prompt international charges of "social dumping" against Japanese products). Since the farmer's family was generally bigger than the laborer's family, per capita income was proportionately even lower. Half the household expenses of the farmer were for food. He had to exert efforts just to stay alive, much less "make a living." The proportion of household expenditures used for food (the Engel coefficient) was reported as 49 for the owner-farmer; 52 for the part-owner, part-tenant; and 57 for the tenant farmer. The low economic level of the farmer served to strengthen the hierarchical structure based on land ownership and to preserve the domination of landlord over tenant farmer. This status hierarchy naturally resulted in differences in the life styles of each class.

During the war production of the most essential item for human needs, *i.e.* food, gave the farmer an opportunity to approach the economic level of households engaged in other industries. Immediately after the war farmers' incomes surpassed that of wage and salary workers. However, with the reconstruction of the economy, farm income once again dropped below other sectors. In 1960 the income of a farmer was 85 percent that of the white-collar worker and 112 percent that of the blue-collar worker. In per capita income the corresponding figures were 65 percent and 87 percent, and farm-family income did not exceed 73 percent of the average income of all wage and salary workers.

The income of farm households began to increase thereafter. In 1972, even the per capita income of a farmer surpassed that of a wage and salary worker; according to 1975 statistics, the income of a farm family was 134 percent that of a wage and salary worker's family, and farm per capita income was 113 percent that of salary workers. Farm workers' Engel coefficient has dropped to below 25. This is lower than the 29 coefficient of urban workers.

Thus the farm family, which before the war had to endure a life of poverty and suppress all cultural aspirations, has now been urbanized to the extent that it can spend two-thirds of its income on things other than food. A less concrete but important shift has also taken place in social attitudes. With a general changeover from tenant to owner as a result of the land reform and the consequent weakening of class distinctions, farmers no longer uncritically accept a different living standard for landlords and tenant farmers. The standard of living for all farm families has become equalized, but additional income stems largely from jobs in other industries as a supplement to inadequate farm income. The per capita share of the family budget is larger in families with small farms of one hectare or less, especially 0.5 hectare or less, as less farmland means that they can devote relatively more time to earning nonfarming income than can farm workers with more land. By 1963 the practice of farm family members taking part-time jobs raised their outside income above their farm income. Moonlighting and working at non-farming jobs has been further encouraged recently by official reluctance to raise government payments to growers for rice and by the policy of discouraging rice production. Nonfarming income is now greater than that from farming. For example, in 1970 the proportion of agricultural income in the total income of farm families dropped to 33 percent; this tendency continued thereafter, and since 1975 it has amounted to less than 30 percent.

Changing economic and social conditions have stimulated the "urbanization" of consumption patterns in farm families, particularly those with stable and substantial incomes from nonfarming jobs. Ordinary farmers, who before the war might have resented the fact that the landlord could buy a radio while they could not, have equipped their homes with television sets. The rate of distribution of TV sets among farmers is almost the same as in the big cities. Most farm families now have electric refrigerators and washing machines, and in recent years there has been a sharp rise in the number who own automobiles; in 1970 the rate of car

Table 15.   Rises in Consumption Levels

		Total	Food	Hous-ing	Util-ities	Cloth-ing	Misc.
1970	Cities	126.7	111.7	145.3	137.4	122.2	137.6
(1965 = 100)	Rural areas	146.9	116.4	143.6	133.6	151.7	182.5
1975	Cities	113.5	103.6	108.8	128.3	104.1	127.4
(1970 = 100)	Rural areas	132.1	111.6	138.2	115.4	115.5	149.2
1979	Cities	107.6	101.9	106.3	115.3	100.9	109.5
(1975 = 100)	Rural areas	111.3	106.2	105.6	117.3	105.4	115.3

ownership surpassed that of urban workers. According to the 1980 statistics, car ownership of urban workers was 54 percent, while that of rural workers was way ahead—74.5 percent. Table 15 shows the rise in levels of consumption during recent years. Taking 1965 as the base year, in 1970 total consumption was 127 for urban and 147 for rural areas; and taking 1970 as the base year, the index numbers for 1975 were 114 and 132, respectively. Although the rate of growth of consumption levels was stagnant in those five years in both cities and rural areas, relative rises in expenditure levels for clothing and miscellaneous expenses were far greater in rural areas than in urban; these were main factors in the rapid rise of consumption level in farm areas.

While the Engel coefficient has dropped, there has also been a tendency to limit expenditures for food in order to buy consumer durables. While this tendency is not limited to rural families, they nevertheless spend a greater proportion of their food outlay for cereals than others do. There are still problems, but the life-style of farm families, including types of clothing, food and shelter, has changed significantly. Farmers now wear Western-style clothes for going out, the women go to beauty parlors just as city women do and children's clothing—something very different from even a generation ago—is indistinguishable from that of city children. Eating habits have also changed; seasoning is no longer limited to soy sauce and bean paste. There has been widespread improvement in dwellings, including kitchens and cooking facilities. As of 1980, 73 percent of all rural communities had water systems, and there were very few hamlets without telephones.

In the old days opportunities for recreation in rural villages were limited to the annual Bon Festival folk dancing and Shinto festivals for the local guardian deity, an occasional village theatrical and relatively frequent gatherings of village fraternities. Now not only has television made recreation an everyday matter, but people also often go to nearby cities for diversion. Group excursions of farmers to other parts of Japan and sometimes even abroad have become common. As a result, there has been a striking increase in cultural and recreational expenditures compared with before the war. In the field of formal education the proportion of students who continue to high school, which was less than 70 percent in 1965, exceeds 90 percent, no different from that of urban youth. The time when an elementary school education was considered sufficient for farm children is now in the distant past.

Farmers once sought their raison d'etre in an ideology that made agriculture the foundation for society and the system of social values in Japan; it was the life-giving occupation, unlike urban occupations, which corrupted and degraded man. Although agriculture was left in the cold by modern industry, being accorded the least favored treatment, it was nevertheless hailed as the foundation of the state. But this glorification of hard work and low standards of living is no longer accepted by the farming population. Farmers today no longer consider consumption a vice and cultural aspirations a luxury. Agriculture is just another business that is expected to produce a profit; hence the growing awareness that it is less rewarding or profitable compared with other sectors.

The overall difficulties facing agriculture in recent years have strengthened this awareness. If farmers find it impossible to lower their present standard of living in spite of the impasse, they will have to reconsider the most basic props in their life-style. Life-style or culture does not change easily, and the present transformation in the life of farmers is by no means a smooth one. Certain aspects lag while others are moving ahead. The purchase of cars and furniture, for example, has stunted development of other undertakings in their lives. The rise in standards of living among farmers has not, therefore, been well balanced or even. Competition based only on vanity or concern for appearances has also affected cultural development. Farmers are, in any case, demanding much more in the realms of recreation, culture and education than ever before.

To follow such pursuits, farm families want to do additional work to supplement farm income. So long as their total agricultural and extra income continues to increase, approaching income levels of wage and salary earners, the overall attitude of farmers toward society and nation may stay unchanged. When this particular group, however, begins to hit a "ceiling" and experiences difficulty in maintaining and raising their new standards of living, both their attitude and their behavior will probably begin to change. Change in political orientations and attitudes toward government may even effect change in political alignment and power. One can speculate that farmers' support for the present government might then weaken sufficiently to force political change, but no such shift will occur quickly, although it has started. Though rural society has undergone great change, in many respects it remains stagnant.

3. Change and Stagnation in Village Society

We have seen how farm families now tend to fall into either the small category of those engaged exclusively in agriculture or the much larger one of those working at additional occupations. Another rural group is the great number of nonfarming families who live in farm villages. A considerable number of settlements have developed in which nonfarming families are in the majority while only a few farm families remain. According to a 1960 worldwide census of agriculture and forestry, the average rural settlement consisted of 39 agricultural households and 25 non-agricultural ones, for a total of 64. But the same census, conducted in 1970, found 37 agricultural households to 44 nonagricultural ones, for a total of 81 in the same average settlement; the 1980 census found 33 agricultural against 108 nonagricultural households, for a total of 141. In all settlements, the average number of nonfarming families rose substantially. But in fact, purely agricultural villages in which farm households are 80 percent or more of the total amounted to half of all rural settlements in 1970, and over 35 percent even in 1980; hence, the average number of nonfarming families exceeding farm families in agricultural villages all over Japan most probably stems from the increase of nonfarming residents in villages around cities. Indeed the nonfarming population in farm villages has increased, and at present farm villages with less than half nonfarming families are reaching 35 percent. In addition 65 percent of "farm families" are engaged in additional occupations similar to those of the nonfarming population. Considering these facts, the rapid breakup of these settlements into heterogeneous units becomes clear. At the same time the social character of these settlements is undergoing striking change.

In the first place, they are no longer close-knit communities encompassing a small area, with more or less determined patterns of class composition. Prewar farm villages varied in composition, including owner-farmers and tenant farmers, or groups of families who worked exclusively in agriculture and those who had additional occupations, but the farm settlement of the past had a design. It centered around the landlords and a class of prominent people next to them who managed production and the life of the settlement as a whole. The breakup of the landlord system, however, has made the formation of common goals difficult in a settlement whose members are divided between those engaged solely in agriculture and the promotion of farm production and those who earn their main income in other industries, farming only for their own food supply and for security in retirement. (A young or middle-aged man will plan to carry on farming after retirement from the other occupation; in the meantime, the farm work will be done by women and old people.) Also, because many nonfarming families now live in farm villages and commute to work simply because they cannot have houses in the town or city, it is difficult to unite all the inhabitants into a community within the framework of the village.

In the second place, differentiation within the rural settlements has been reinforced by external stimuli. Links with outside society have become stronger since the war, and the life of the villagers has become more varied and far-ranging. The development of agricultural production for the commercial market and the rise in consumption have forged new ties between village and city, while the growing numbers of farmers who take other jobs, some of whom commute to the cities, have created a steady urban-rural interchange. Furthermore, mergers that were effected under the 1953 Law to Promote the Consolidation of Towns and Villages superseded a town and village system dating back to 1889. The law of 1953 was enacted in a profoundly different environment from that of the middle Meiji period, and the new municipalities were several times larger than their predecessors, while villages on the outskirts of a city were incorporated into the central city. Thus they virtually became urban areas that were part of the same administrative district and formed a single local self-governing body. As the bonds between city and village grew stronger, one could no longer speak of a purely rural society living by means of agriculture. The idea of being "cut off" from the city has become inconceivable today.

Another agent of change is the location of industry. The drawbacks of overcrowded industrial facilities have begun to outweigh the advantages of concentration. When the dispersal of industry and the formation of new industrial regions is carried out through regional development plans, decisive changes will take place in the structure of rural villages within such a region. It is possible that rural settlements will be completely broken up or left with only vestiges of what they were. This trend is conspicuous now in only a relatively few rural villages, but small industries everywhere, seeking factory sites where land and labor are cheap, are hoping to move into the rural areas. In addition to "urban sprawl" and the urban housing shortage, industrial relocation is changing the entire aspect of rural village society.

The degree of structural change in village society differs according to region, but in all cases the prewar rural village is breaking up. The controlling power of the traditional group within the village has weakened. The neighborhood groups which were once active

in all aspects of village life have become merely the final trans-
mission points of administration. The functions of the cooperative
organization for assisting with funeral services have been reduced.
With the decline of religious faith and the abundance of recreational opportunities, religious associations, too, are becoming
shadows of what they used to be. Of the groups formed after the
Meiji town and village system went into effect, the young men's
associations and the women's leagues have declined the most; the
latter find it difficult even to stay in existence. The organizations
which are replacing them—the Agricultural Cooperatives' (*Nō-
kyō*) young men's and women's divisions—also find it difficult to
function. The diversification of the farm families has weakened
the function of the Agricultural Practice Union (*Nōji Jikkō
Kumiai*). Instead, industry-oriented associations of fruit growers,
dairy farmers, chicken and hog raisers and cooperative shipping
organizations, cutting across village lines and unrelated to any
one village unit, have become the key administrative and commercial facilities for farmers. The era when the members of a
village, regardless of occupation, formed a single community and
cooperated in all aspects of its life, when the village itself controlled
and regulated its inhabitants—that era is a thing of the past.

Nevertheless, villagers have not been freed from the traditions
of the village and its groups. Village control of water is still considered necessary for paddy cultivation, for example. The effect of
these traditions has been a failure to develop rationally organized
groups operating as independently functioning bodies to meet
specific group needs apart from the village. The "village" has not
become just another organization; its all-encompassing authority
is still recognized, at least in theory.

Traditions of the past are deeply rooted in the structure and
operation of village self-government. The idea that local affairs
should be handled by the villagers themselves has left a wide
margin for village self-government alongside municipal self-
government. It is considered a duty for each family to share the
burden of village expenses and to contribute equal amounts of
volunteer labor for community work. Village official positions
have lost their prestige and are considered merely troublesome
and unremunerative, and no movement has developed toward a

democratic or egalitarian reform of the method of selecting officers nor of the operation of self-government.

Economically, agriculture should be divorced from the village itself and run by specialized organizations set up for specific purposes. The village will then become an entity whose purpose is to promote the common interests and welfare of its inhabitants, regardless of whether they be farm or nonfarming families, but at present the gap between the two—agriculture and village—is simply glossed over. There is no clear-cut division of functions between them, despite the growing heterogeneity of village inhabitants and the need for different modes of organization. Yet the old-time "village spirit" survives: the attitudes that made solidarity and tranquillity the goals of village society and that gave priority to the common interests of those living in it.

Thus the village continues to emphasize communal interests over class interest even after it has been incorporated into the broader municipal self-government. Its behavior is governed by the "village first" principle—the old principle of giving priority to the interests of one's own town or village that dates back to the preconsolidation era. The emphasis on local interests becomes the basis of town and village politics and affects the way farmers relate to prefectural and national governments. It strengthens the role of the prefectural assembly and Diet members as intermediaries between villagers and prefectural or national government. Old political attitudes, therefore, and the tendency to push action through representatives persist. In this respect village society has still not clearly emerged from the way of life of the old village community. Startling change has occurred against the background of tenacious traditions.

4. Disintegration of the Traditional Community

The rural village is now confronted with the dissolution of the communal type of organization that has persisted despite rising waves of industrialization. Little is being done to try to reorganize it, however; despite the new variety in class and occupational composition and new breadth of interests, the political and administrative aspects of local self-government are almost unchanged from the time when the village was a communal type of self-sufficient unit.

The formation of autonomous democratic communities that can replace the old communal structure requires acknowledgment of the many different, and even conflicting, interests that now coexist in it, and the organization of groups appropriate to their various functions. The functions of the village (*buraku*) itself should be curtailed or streamlined, and to elicit the cooperation necessary to a small local community, the village should be run according to the principle of fair and impartial sharing of benefits and burdens. A community of the smallest unit (such as *buraku*) is of course inadequate to stand alone as a modern community. The viable community should probably equal the average school district, with a community center and facilities necessary for daily life. The inhabitants of a rural district should demand this minimum standard from the municipal government. It could perhaps be expanded into a second type of community that would include an urban or town area, and even to a third type, the "rurban" community. If each of these different-sized communities can fulfill appropriate functions and each kind is organized to respond to the desires of the residents, the traditional rural village will have been replaced with a new community, and the old communal consciousness will develop into a sense of independent solidarity.

To achieve an organic relationship of city, town and village, and to achieve balanced development, the present municipal governments must develop new goals and methods beyond simply effective capital investment. The policy to encourage factory location in the environs of the urban section imposes troubles and suffering on the rural section; the first and second types of communities could not develop, and even the third type could not become a true community if concern for social development stops with the central sections of urban areas.

The same is true of regional development. To reexamine exactly what is meant by "region," one can see that balanced development cannot occur only from the growth of the central district, nor can it stop with increased benefits only to certain upper classes or groups. A region will "develop" and flourish when the life of

IV. The Growth of Urban Society

1. Increase of Cities and Urban Growth

As far back as the 17th century Japan's cities, such as Edo (Tokyo), Kyoto and Osaka, were among the largest cities in the world. The urban population at the time of the Meiji Restoration in 1868 was, nonetheless, less than 10 percent of the national total. Even as late as 1920, when the first national census was conducted, the urban population had not reached 20 percent. The following quarter-century reflected the growth of capitalism in a rapid increase in the number of cities; their population grew to nearly 40 percent of the total.

The Pacific War brought a stop to this trend. Immediately after the end of the war a steady flow of population back to the rural areas reduced urban population to less than 30 percent. Even by 1950 it was considerably less than 40 percent. From the mid-fifties,

Table 16. Population (in thousands) of Cities of 100,000 or More and Its Percentage of Total Population

	1960			1970			1980		
	Cities	Population	%	Cities	Population	%	Cities	Population	%
1,000,000–	6	16,688	17.9	8	20,856	19.9	10	23,296	19.9
500,000–	3	1,804	1.9	7	4,562	4.4	9	5,742	4.9
300,000–	12	4,262	4.6	21	7,890	7.5	36	13,709	11.7
200,000–	21	5,375	5.5	41	10,078	9.6	42	10,345	8.8
100,000–	71	9,914	10.6	73	10,416	10.0	96	12,965	11.1
Total Population		94,302	100.0		104,665	100.0		117,057	100.0

however, the economy began to shift from restoration to growth, and cities gradually returned to prewar levels of population. Thereafter they entered a period of rapid growth. From 1950 to 1960 population steadily gravitated to the large cities; as we have already seen, the areas of cities peripheral to large metropolises began to expand after 1960. Both the number and size of cities have grown remarkably. Merely having city status as administrative units does not necessarily qualify a city as an urban center, yet if a city with a population of 100,000 or more is taken to be an urban center, then urban center population in 1960 amounted to 41 percent of the total population, became 52 percent in 1970, and then reached 56 percent in 1980 (see Table 16). In other words, more than half the population today lives in metropolitan areas. If we add the population of municipal corporations of 50,000 or more to this number, the proportion amounts to 68.5 percent.

Modern Japanese cities have typically developed as consumer cities, evolving out of castle towns of the Tokugawa period to become prefectural capitals after the Meiji Restoration. Needless to say, there are newly developed cities which were agricultural or fishing villages in the Tokugawa period. Such industrial cities as Yawata, Kawasaki and Hitachi, which developed only after the Restoration, are good examples of that pattern. Others, such as Yokohama, Niigata and Aomori, which grew into important cities after the opening of ports to foreign trade, also developed into prefectural capitals. Most of Japan's cities, however, originally developed out of political or administrative centers, whose populations later increased with the growth of industry. The same pattern has repeated itself often in the postwar growth of cities, as well.

The formal administrative structure of Japan duly recognizes local autonomy and decentralization of authority, but in fact functions to centralize authority on both the national and prefectural levels. Thus, along with the concentration of population in Tokyo, the population in prefectural capitals has also expanded. Even in recent years many cities, by virtue of being political centers, have continued to attract more people and develop industry in the outskirts.

The main trend in rapid urban growth, however, has been expansion of industrial, rather than political, centers. The shift from coal to oil as a source of power has had a particularly great influence on the location of industry, through the formation of large petro-chemical complexes in areas close to existing industrial regions. The complexes have accelerated rapid urbanization in such areas.

Another factor in Japan's urban growth is the great number of new cities recently sprung into existence. As is generally known, consolidation of towns and villages after the war extended the scope of municipalities, doubled their number, and created innumerable cities. Yet many of these were nothing more than small towns that included adjacent or nearby farm villages spread over a fairly wide area. Another type of new city includes those which developed more recently in the outskirts of the large cities as a result of the sudden population increase in towns and smaller cities within the metropolitan area. It is the increase in number and rapid growth of this kind of city which accounts for the fact that while population growth in the six largest cities has come to a standstill, the populations of the metropolitan areas are still rapidly growing.

The overall conclusions to be drawn from the rapid growth of urban population are: first, the large cities are already overcrowded and, because of high land prices that stem from an inappropriate official land policy, they are approaching the limits of population growth. Without a drastic program of urban reconstruction and redevelopment, such limitations cannot be overcome.

Second, all regional urban centers are growing, but growth is especially marked in those which are also industrial cities.

Third, the old industrial cities expanded as the economy grew, and the new manufacturing-industrial cities, especially in the Pacific coastal belt, were among the fastest growing. From 1963 onward the development of new industrial cities pushed the spread of such cities beyond the Pacific coastal zone. Among the latter are cities built where formerly there were nothing but farming or fishing villages, thus creating urban areas very suddenly.

Fourth, and this is related to the first and second trends, urbanization is also taking place on the periphery of regional central cities, as in the outskirts of large cities. This may be considered characteristic of recent urban trends—the expansion of urban society.

Thus, rapid city growth is taking place not as population expansion in established urban areas and redevelopment of existing facilities and installations, but in a mushrooming kind of expansion which is rapidly taking over areas which were once only rural villages. In other words, the rapid growth of cities is swiftly turning Japan into an urban society; villages are literally being "citified." The dynamism of urbanization is spreading throughout Japan as a whole and consequently throughout the life of the Japanese people, even those who are living in what are still rural community areas.

For more than seventy years after the Meiji Restoration Japanese encouraged more and bigger cities, at a rate that was rapid even by world standards. Nevertheless, Japan remained essentially a rural society; its social system and the fundamental character of the dominating political trends were rural. Each family was responsible for its own livelihood, and social life was the responsibility of the community. There was little interest in the social institutions and public facilities necessary in an urban society. Political patterns and thinking were geared to assumptions that were valid when the traditional community prevailed. They have remained fundamentally unchanged since the end of the war. To augment national wealth and military strength, prewar Japan concentrated almost exclusively on the development of industy and showed almost no concern for developing the institutions and facilities for life in an urban environment or for social guarantees of the people's livelihood. After the war economic growth became the single most important national goal, pushing all other considerations aside. It spurred industrialization on at an even more rapid pace, and resulted in unbalanced and unplanned urban growth. The imbalances in urban life have been allowed to run their course, and industrialization and urbanization have, therefore, progressed in an even more uncontrolled manner. The process has become a vicious circle that seems doomed to repetition. The cities of Japan have today reached a point where many aspects of urban life will be destroyed if nothing is done to control their growth.

2. Oversized and Overcrowded Cities

The development of the old castle town represents the typical growth pattern of the Japanese city. As the seat of local political authority, it was built according to a plan which accommodated the interests of the feudal lord. It did not just grow spontaneously; it was formed with a plan and a system. It was not, however, built to suit the needs of the inhabitants; almost no cities were formed as a result of their citizens' exercise of the right of self-determination.

From the Meiji Restoration on, cities grew larger, but without the tradition of popular government or any concept of city planning behind them. Streets, which were originally laid out with an eye to defense strategy, were not organized or reconstructed, and when a city began to expand, the street and block layout did not expand according to rational planning but simply in response to immediate changes and concrete, short-term needs. Many people became aware of the wastefulness and harm of such unplanned, disorderly build-up of cities, but measures to rectify the uncontrolled spread were makeshift, with no relevance to long-range, larger problems. Some cities were carefully planned; Sapporo is one good example, but it is the exception rather than the rule among all Japanese cities. Installation of water supply systems in the cities was a matter of course, but sewage systems did not merit the same treatment because traditional agriculture included use of night soil in fields as fertilizer. City planning, as an all-embracing concept for urban living, remained immature for a long time.

Most of the cities that grew in this unplanned, spontaneous way were reduced to rubble by bombing during World War II. This disaster presented an excellent opportunity for planned postwar reconstruction of the major cities, including Tokyo, but for the most part the opportunity was not fully utilized. Cities were restored along the old lines, even as the economy began to grow and greater crowds of people were drawn into the cities. The influx into the larger ones was sudden and extreme. Added to the lack of any overall land policy to manage the new situation was the fact that growing population levels made land prices soar rapidly. Even belated street-widening programs required large sums to acquire land, and these programs placed a heavy burden on city finances.

Any basic, planned reconstruction of the cities appeared almost hopeless; so, as they became too large, they also suffered from overcrowding.

In the unplanned, disorderly development of Japanese cities, residences were located among industrial sites where they were directly exposed to the soot spewed out by factory chimneys. Factories had grown up here and there in a haphazard manner, and none had any idea of cooperating with others to control water pollution caused by industrial waste. It was also a matter of course for them to pump the water they needed from underground sources; this pumping, over a long period of time and with no controls by any government agency, caused the ground to sink. Thus, the cities suffered not only industrial pollution but also other, less immediately visible damage to the environment by industry. As the cities became larger and more dense, the damage became all the greater.

In addition to industrial pollution and all its ramifications, Japanese cities also face problems of "urban pollution" that get worse as a city grows. Deficient sewage systems make the disposal of human waste a serious problem. Even in the outlying areas of Tokyo, vacuum pump trucks are still used to pump out septic tanks a—phenomenon unimaginable in Western cities. The enormous amounts of trash, furthermore, and the lack of adequate dumping grounds have created frictions among residents that authorities call the "garbage wars." Tokyo is, in the long run, more like a big village than a modern industrial capital.

The need for park areas and playgrounds, something that does not arise in a rural community, has not been given serious consideration in the cities. As a result, urban Japan is incomparably poorer in parks and open areas than most countries in the world. At first glance Tokyo may seem to have numerous green areas, but actually it has no more than 1.2 square meters of park area per capita, and even the cities with larger park areas such as Kobe and Nagoya have less than 3.0 square meters, while London has 22.8, New York 19.2, and Berlin 24.7. Where individual households cannot, for lack of space, have yards and gardens, public facilities must include parks, greenbelts and tree-lined streets. When open space in a city is too limited, it becomes entirely unsuitable for family living and the bringing up of children.

As a result of the rise in standards of living, heating and air-conditioning equipment is gradually coming into general use. Because more and more people have decided they need and can afford such utilities, the living environment of the cities has grown worse. When coal was used for heating, soot and smoke were problems. Now oil has replaced coal, to create greater air pollution, while the water needed for air conditioning removes more water from underground, and the ground continues to sink. The idea of air-conditioning and heating facilities to serve a whole group of dwelling units has not been put into practice. The addition of wastes from each individual unit compounds the smoke rising from industrial districts within the city and filling urban skies with greater concentrations of fumes. The widespread use of individual air conditioners likewise overloads electrical circuits and compounds the problem of sinking land.

Lack of planning has also resulted in traffic jams on city streets because of the sudden increase in the number of automobiles. In spite of the high price of land cities have been widening streets and building expressways, but even so they have not caught up with the increasing automobile traffic. Congestion is not letting up, despite improvement in the roads, while automobile exhaust has created the serious problem of photochemical smog. The larger the city is, the greater the pollution, and the more densely populated it is, the greater the damage.

When the key functions of a city are concentrated in its center, as in Japan, traffic into the city becomes all the more congested and unorganized. The city center absorbs huge numbers of people during the day, most of whom leave the city at night. They commute from the suburbs and from new residential districts and apartment complexes spreading out from the suburbs to satellite cities and farther. This has produced dense rush-hour traffic congestion and an increase in serious or fatal traffic accidents. No matter how much urban traffic regulation is improved, it cannot keep pace with the increase in commuter population. A great deal of energy is also used up by commuters riding jam-packed trains during rush hours.

The problems of urban overpopulation have become intolerable today. During the mid-sixties, when there was no easy answer to the concentration of population in the big cities, the conditions seemed to indicate that, though a city might be very large, it could be tolerated if it were not also overcrowded. But the amount of investment necessary to create a large city without a dense population would be astronomical. Excessive urban growth should be restrained; efforts must be made to limit the size of smaller cities and scale down those that have become uncontrollably large and overcrowded.

Uncomfortable, destructive overcrowding has given rise to the idea of the "civil minimum" in cities, the demand that certain standards of living be made, possible by provision of a minimum level of public welfare, facilities and utilities. To establish and maintain these levels is certainly not easy, but it is of vital importance to all our cities.

Overcrowding has become so intolerable that urban dwellers' attitudes have begun to change. Most of the population of a large city once came from regional districts. Even today many come from families in outlying areas and stream out of the city at the time of the August Bon Festival and at New Year's. However, though such people still return "home" for the holidays, they no longer consider themselves temporary residents of the city. Moreover, in the hundred-years-plus since the Meiji Restoration, the number of people born in the city has naturally increased. The urban populace by and large consider themselves permanent residents and for that reason they are deeply concerned about improvement of the present intolerable urban environment. The election of many reform-minded mayors and governors has its roots in the new attitudes of residents toward overcrowded, large cities. Any solution, however, lies well beyond the capabilities of local governments. It will depend on basic shifts in the thinking of the national government, which will undoubtedly have to help.

3. Imbalances in Urbanization

Rapid urban growth is everywhere evident: in suburban and new housing development areas in the vicinity of the large cities, in the suburbs of regional central cities and in districts adjacent to new industrial cities. What were once rural areas are beginning to appear urban; country villages have come to the city.

Rural areas now being "developed" once had almost no urban facilities. They are being invaded and turned into residential districts in an ad hoc, unplanned way. What was rural landscape quickly becomes a complex of apartment buildings, which often do not bring with them any planned development of public facilities. This has been especially true of the newly developed housing districts that are eating away at the countryside near almost every city of significant size. It appears that builders are just trying to increase the number of places where people might sleep. If they were to go so far as to install a water system and pave the roads, residents would have no grounds for demanding more. Such precipitous urbanization, like the earlier formation of cities, is creating densely crowded residential districts which suffer from a disorderly setting that is neither rural nor urban. The concrete structures may be arranged in a regular pattern and present the aspect of a new city, but except for the apartment complexes themselves there is little that can be called "urban."

The people who fill these new urban developments are relatively young, unable to bear much of the city's tax burden, and yet with children of school age. The newly urbanized municipality is beset with demands to lay water systems, build roads and elementary schools and enlarge junior high schools. There are insufficient surplus funds to establish other facilities necessary for an urban society. The local municipality, restricted by the rise in land prices and hard pressed even to buy land for an elementary school, has no latitude for planned development of parks, playgrounds or green areas. It is unable to create such areas now or to secure the necessary land for them even in the future. Thus, residents of newly urbanized districts are at the double disadvantage of having to commute long distances to work as well as having to put up with the inadequacies of their environment at home.

Japanese have had no experience in planned city construction, and the government has given all its attention to economic growth, leaving the expansion of cities to the mercies of immediate changes and needs. The growth of the economy has stimulated the building of more new dwelling units, but government assistance has taken care of only 45 percent at most. Most of the initiative has been left to the independent efforts of private builders who have had neither a central coordinating agency nor the incentive to plan their projects within any overall framework.

Hence the uncontrolled, undirected urban sprawl. The concept of a "new town" like those in England, with work sites and residences located in the same area, is still undeveloped in Japan. Nor has the government seriously attempted to scatter its agencies more widely to prevent cities from becoming too big. The construction of the new academic city at Tsukuba is an exception, but even in this case inadequate funds have delayed the schedule of work and give a clear indication of the passive, or negative, attitude held by the national government toward the construction of new cities.

Those who work in large cities and central regional cities have become resigned to commuting long distances and living in areas where they can afford the relatively lower land prices. As a result, they are scattered throughout many districts in the metropolitan areas and have few "residential" advantages. Construction of apartment complexes of the public housing type is also restricted by high land prices, and builders are unable to find locations consistent with good planning. It is said that since 1955, city land prices have risen by 27 times, and those in large cities by more than 31 times. The nominal wages of the urban employee have in the same time period increased by only about 7 times. When higher construction costs are added, building one's own home has become an impossibility for many. The inability of most to build or buy their own homes naturally makes crowding inevitable. Those whose applications for public housing are accepted are said to be lucky, for the waiting lists are long, but despite the fact that Japan is a great economic power, it is difficult to save enough to move from public housing to one's own home. So people buy cars and go for drives on their days off to forget their frustrations.

The fact that some people are looking for a second house even though they do not own their first one has its roots in land speculation and the desire to escape polluted cities. For most people living in newly urbanized districts the possibility of owning a second house is perhaps unthinkable, but if second-home ownership is becoming fairly common, it is only because Japan's urbanization has been so distorted and because rise in land prices may go on indefinitely.

The impossibility of developing urban facilities in pace with the progress of urbanization applies also to the newly developing areas and the new industrial cities program. After an initial period of favorable treatment, newly established industrial plants increase city revenues, mostly through payment of property taxes. This raises hopes of more building or of expanding urban facilities. Up to now, however, these hopes usually have not become reality. Priority in the allotment of tax revenues is given to installations around industrial districts and to facilities connected with factories; otherwise, they go into the "cosmetic" expenditures—decorations that give the city an outward urban appearance—or they are spent on preventive and restorative activities to offset the effects of pollution. Consequently, few funds are available to raise urban living conditions to acceptable modern standards. The cost of facilities connected with industrial plants should be borne by the enterprises that benefit from them, and anti-pollution measures should be the responsibility of the polluters. Ironically, however, it is the city governments that have had to carry the burden, either because their legislatures give priority to the interests of the industrial plants or because they were the ones who invited industry in the first place.

The benefits accruing to local landowners from this kind of urbanization have been huge, due to the rise in land prices. Some suddenly become wealthy merely because their ancestors happened to own land in a given area; values go up not as a result of any efforts on their part but because of changes in social and economic conditions. Ideally, a proportion of the profit from this price rise should be returned to society as a sort of capital gains tax, and society should use it to compensate those who were forced to give up farming by the encroachment of the city, so that they might continue to live at their accustomed level. Since no such compensation will be soon forthcoming, the owner is entitled to get the highest price possible for his land. The national government itself encourages this trend when, in compensating for land expropriated for a dam or an expressway, it allows reluctant land-

owners to reap extra gains. The leap in land prices which this produces has become a serious barrier to further social development
in Japan. It has also violated people's sense of fair play and frustrated their hopes for a better life.

4. Structural Changes in Urban Society

Most Japanese cities were essentially consumption centers.
Their main attractions were shopping areas and arcades. As these
cities became large metropolises, the central shopping arcades
often developed into modern shopping centers, whose owners and
employees might live elsewhere, though more often than not they
retained the pattern of street-floor shops with residences above
them. The side and back streets were usually packed with multiple
dwellings built close together.

Such downtown shopping districts retained a social structure
somewhat like that of a rural village. Those who worked and
lived in one locality spent all their time with others in the same
shopping district. Authority in the neighborhood association
(*chōnaikai*), which lumped together the shopping street and its side
and back streets, was held by influential shopowners and the owners of small factories scattered among the shops. Those with the
most power were elected ward and city assemblymen; some of
these men had ties with members of prefectural assemblies or
the national Diet. Such local leaders might show no interest in
national political issues, but they felt some pressure to take part in
activities affecting the interests of their own community and gradually came to believe that they were the main force in politics.
Neither the local bosses nor the assemblymen had any idea of
raising the level of urban living as a whole, but they showed great
zeal in such matters as street or gutter repairs; indeed, their activities as "gutter-cover assemblymen" were remarkable. The
vote-getting apparatus which these local assemblyman could
muster at the grass-roots level assured conservative support in the
downtown districts.

In this respect the new suburban districts were similar. Their
residents had little interest in their communities—which they con-

sidered little more than "bed-towns"—and while few former villagers remained, a handful of them rose to influential status as small and independent entrepreneurs. These erstwhile farmers often dominated local politics. Comparing the upper-middle class residential districts, such as the Yamanote area in central Tokyo, with the suburban districts of regional cities, we find more similarities than differences. The bulk of the population of these residential districts consists of white-collar workers commuting to their jobs and living in scattered isolation from one another. They leave the management of the old neighborhood associations to members of the old middle class, made up mainly of the owners of independent enterprises in the small shopping districts found in each area. The main difference between a high-class residential section and the typical downtown area is that the former consists of upper-income families that have few demands to make, since the environment itself is good. On the whole, they are indifferent to local municipal government.

Where cities emerged as large enterprises were established, in many cases company housing was provided, but living in company housing did not separate the worker from his place of work. Such integrated areas tended to take on the characteristics of a village even though the dwellings were modern. The paternalistic employee welfare policies made the company housing area a special district, isolated from the rest of the city. The company provided athletic fields, playgrounds, and shops and hospitals for the employees and their families. For example, in the city of Hitachi the company housing area used to be referred to as "inside the fence," as opposed to the rest of society "outside the fence." "Inside" employees felt completely detached from the other world in the same city, made no demands on the city as a whole, and had no interest in it. In spite of the fact that the new middle and working classes were together creating a larger city, it was run mainly by the old middle class. This kind of structure clearly prevented even gradual modernization of Japanese cities.

Since the war, and especially in recent years, however, the rapid growth of cities has brought about changes in this structure. As we have seen from the make-up of the population by industry, the new middle and working classes have been growing. The prospects for the class of independent commercial proprietors, who were once the masters of consumption-oriented cities, have become much bleaker. The household-industry type of tiny factory scattered around the heart of the city is dying out, and the future of those that still exist is dark. The old middle class formed by these small proprietors is also rapidly diminishing.

The expansion of consumer demand in a growing economy has pushed commercial activity steadily upward, in terms of number of stores, persons employed, amount of sales or any other index. The increase has been most conspicuous in wholesale trade, department stores and supermarkets. Other general retail businesses, however, while their numbers and volume of transactions have increased, are enjoying a relatively smaller share of commerce as a whole. Commerce cannot be mechanized like manufacturing industry, and throughout the world small shops continue to exist. But compared to small shops in the advanced countries of the West, those in Japan are really tiny; the percentage of enterprises employing only family members is particularly high. The sudden rise in wages and the worker shortage have added to the pressures already exerted on most of these shops by the inroads of department and self-service stores. They are up against excessive competition. Before the war such a shopowner could hire an employee at low wages and later help him open a shop of his own. Moreover, it was relatively easy to find somone to work long hours in the shop from early morning until late at night.

That pattern is now a thing of the past. The small shops cannot compete with the large ones and are steadily falling behind. Change in the structure of commerce has heightened the difference in interests between large shopowners and small shopowners, at the same time pushing their political sentiments far apart. Some owners of these insecure, small shops are abandoning their long-time support of the conservative party. An increasing number are becoming members of the lay organization of Nichiren Shōshū, Sōkagakkai, or they are joining organizations of democratic commerce and industry associations *(minshu shōkōkai)* aligned with the Communist party. This has complicated the political structure of the doyens of the shopping arcades, which were once thoroughly conservative and controlled by the old middle class. Along with the

Table 17. Percentage Distribution of Shops by Number of Employees (1979)

Number of employees	Wholesale	Retail	Wholesale & retail
1 – 2	21.6	61.1	53.9
3 – 4	25.0	24.0	24.2
5 – 9	28.5	10.5	13.8
10 – 19	14.8	2.8	5.0
20 – 29	4.5	0.8	1.4
30 – 49	3.1	0.5	1.0
50 – 99	1.8	0.2	0.5
100 –	0.7	0.1	0.2

residents of rural villages they used to form the basic support for the conservative forces. The larger a city becomes, the more politically heterogeneous its downtown areas become.

The inflated new middle class and the working class either live crowded together in small privately built apartments located here and there in old urban areas or are scattered in apartment complexes and new residential districts. In either case they are free of the control of the old middle class. Paying high rents for one-room apartments in small wooden apartment houses, they simply wait for the chance to escape from there. They have no interest whatever in neighborhood affairs. Residents of apartment complexes and new residential districts are also breaking away from conservative domination by local bosses. Those living in the apartment complexes, in particular, have begun to form apartment complex councils (*danchi jichikai,* "self-government associations") that are quite different from the old neighborhood associations. They have acquired a solid awareness of their rights and through these councils are pressuring the municipal governments for the facilities they need to maintain adequate living conditions. The makeshift measures of a "gutter-cover assemblyman" and the old neighborhood association can no longer fulfill the needs of these new communities.

Structural changes in urban society, as we have seen, have been major factors in the emergence of reformist governments in the large cities. Because of the traditionally heterogeneous pattern of residence in Japanese cities, local domination by the old middle class was tenacious and was for the most part supported by city residents. But economic growth has brought radical change to the social apparatus that maintained this old middle class. Now breaking up, the commanding position of its leaders has weakened. City residents have gradually become aware of the low state of urban environment. Urban and industrial pollution have exacerbated dissatisfaction among new middle and working class residents, and the past few years have seen frequent concerted actions by residents on various problems. It would seem that under such circumstances election of more reformist leaders would be a matter of course. However, the vote-getting power of the conservative downtown leaders still persists, even though their hold has been weakened. Though transient segments of the city's population are not influenced by them and may elect reformist governors and mayors, the power of these local leaders still shows up in the elections for ward and city assemblymen. The voting strength of the transient population is, then, fragmented. In medium-sized and small cities where the voting power of newcomers or transients is still weak, conservative leaders are secure. While there have been fundamental structural changes in Japanese cities as a whole, they have hardly become reformist.

V. Industrialization and Changes in the Working Environment

1. Postwar Industrial Development

Between 1955 and 1960 Japan's gross national product rose by 68 percent. From 1960 to 1970 it doubled every five years, in 1970 reaching an amount 6.7 times that of 1955. Industrial production, which increased 7.6 times during those fifteen years, accounted for the bulk of this growth. Table 18 illustrates the rapid progress of industrialization; apart from 1962 and 1965, the growth rate never was less than 10 percent. Thus, almost every year the growth rate of industrial production has exceeded that of the gross national product. During the 1970s, however, the "dollar shock" in 1971 and the 1973 oil crisis pulled down the rate of economic growth, giving the Japanese economy no choice but to shift to a steady

Table 18. Growth Rates in Industrial Production and Gross National Product (%)

	1960	61	62	63	64	65	66	67	68	69	70
Industrial production	22.5	18.4	4.9	16.2	12.5	3.1	17.1	18.2	15.1	16.7	10.8
Gross national product	12.5	13.5	6.4	12.5	10.6	5.7	11.1	13.1	12.7	11.0	10.4

	71	72	73	74	75	76	77	78	79	80
Industrial production	2.0	10.2	13.5	–9.4	–3.6	10.8	3.2	7.0	9.3	4.7
Gross national product	7.3	9.8	6.4	–0.3	3.4	5.1	5.3	5.2	5.5	5.0

type of growth. At any rate, it can be said that the high growth of the economy all the way through the sixties changed the industrial structure of Japan a great deal.

The growth of heavy and chemical industries was especially striking. Within this category, machinery production doubled between 1960–65, and by 1970 it had tripled. That means a six-fold increase over a ten-year period. The steel industry increased production 4.2 times, and the chemical industry rose 3.6 times. Textile and food processing industries also more than doubled production during this period, but the main factor in the rapidly rising productivity was the development of heavy and chemical industries. Steel and chemical industries showed approximately 30 percent growth even after 1970, while the textile industry registered a slight drop. As a result, the textile industry, which used to be the mainstay of Japanese industry, dropped to less than 10 percent of total industrial production while heavy and chemical industries were accounting for 70 percent. Heavy industry alone, as a result of the sudden leap in machinery production, has jumped almost 50 percent.

As discussed in Chapter I, rapid industrial development caused great changes in the structure of Japan's population. A look at today's working population by industry shows that primary industries employ only 11 percent; secondary industries account for about 34 percent, and tertiary indusries for more than 50 percent. The tables related to population distribution by industry show, along with the sharp drop in numbers engaged in primary industries, more people in secondary industry; the greatest increase, however, has been in the tertiary industries. Thus, as industrialization progresses, the number of people engaged in secondary industries increases, but when a certain stage is reached this trend slows down and their proportion to the total population drops. At the same time, the proportion of those engaged in tertiary industries continues to rise. The reason for these trends is that, as the secondary industries benefit from technological innovations and production increases with greater efficiency, labor requirements decrease. In contrast, the tertiary industries require a larger and larger labor force to maintain a greater production flow.

Although the percentage of the population engaged in tertiary industries has become quite large, Japan still does not resemble the advanced economies of the West in the composition of its population by industry. As we have seen, Japan's commercial world includes many small, independently owned enterprises, a high proportion of whose employees are members of the owner's family. But technical innovations have been introduced into tertiary industries as a whole, including commerce. One illustration of the progress in technology is the introduction of computers, which are now widely used in the finance and insurance businesses. This is also true in commerce and the service industries, in which very small businesses are common. Distribution mechanisms and channels have also been affected by mass production and mass consumption. Larger shops are increasing, for example. Supermarkets, which began to appear in 1955, proliferated from 1960 on. Associated retail stores, such as the "big stores" and the voluntary chain stores, are also increasing, and installment-plan buying is spreading rapidly.

In such fields as agriculture and commerce there are still small independent enterprises operated by the owners or members of their families. But what is remarkable is the increase in the proportion of employees in the total working population. As we have already seen, in 1955 this exceeded the prewar level of 40 percent; in 1960 it rose to more than half; and at present over 70 percent of those gainfully employed are employees.

This proportion still falls below that of advanced Western countries, but it demonstrates how industrialization in postwar Japan has changed the structure of society. In any effort to comprehend modern Japanese society, analysis of rural villages and cities should not overlook the problems of employees. Under what conditions do they work? How does their work affect them? What problems do they have? The answers to these questions are important for a deeper understanding of the various problems of modern Japanese society.

2. Dual Structure of the Economy

A capitalist economy rapidly flourished in Japan following the Meiji Restoration. In the course of this growth huge financial conglomerates, *zaibatsu,* were formed. But along with the *zaibatsu* there remained many small enterprises. This structure still exists in spite of the liquidation of the *zaibatsu* after the war and the rapid postwar economic growth. Japan's economy still rests on a dual structure of monopoly capital and small enterprise.

The extent of monopoly control in certain sectors can be seen from a glance. The three top banks make one-third of all loans; the ten top companies control over 80 percent of the money market. Apart from the plate glass and beer industries where a single company covers half or more of the business, major industries in which over half the business is in the hands of the three largest companies include chemical textiles, newsprint, pig iron, blister steel, aluminum, copper, automobiles and cameras; the ten largest companies produce almost all the pig iron, newsprint and automobiles. The share of the three largest companies in petroleum refining, ammonium sulfate and cement exceeds 40 percent, and that of the ten largest companies in those industries comes to over 80 percent.

While there is a high level of monopoly control in Japan's economy, small enterprises—the other component of the dual structure—are very numerous. As shown in Table 19, the percentage of people working in plants employing 500 or more increased slightly from that of 1955, but those working in small plants employing under 50 still account for over 40 percent of the total. The proportion working in large enterprises of 1,000 or more is still about 16 percent. Comparing this proportion to the approxi-

Table 19. Percentages of Employees by Size of the Manufacturing Plants in Which They Work

	Number of workers				
	−49	−99	−499	−999	1,000−
1957	49.8	10.3	18.9	6.5	14.6
1963	44.5	10.8	21.2	7.6	15.9
1969	44.3	10.7	21.1	8.0	15.9
1975	44.6	11.0	21.0	7.8	15.6

mately 30 percent in America and the nearly 40 percent in West Germany, we see that Japan remains a country of medium and small enterprises. If we compare Japan, where over half the workers are in plants employing less than 100, with West Germany and America, where the proportion is less than 20 percent and 25 percent, respectively, small enterprises loom even larger in our economy. While Japan has enterprises that rank with the biggest in the world, small enterprises still comprise a large proportion of its industry. The proportion is decreasing, but many small enterprises continue to exist; and even though they are engaged in a fiercely competitive struggle for survival as subcontractors to the large central enterprises, they are still a major support to the growth of the economy.

Table 20. Wage Differentials by Size of Plant (Manufacturing Industry)*

| | Number of workers | | | |
	5–29	30–99	100–499	500–
1955	—	58.8	74.3	100.0
1960	46.3	58.9	70.7	100.0
1965	63.2	71.1	80.9	100.0
1970	61.8	69.6	81.4	100.0
1975	59.8	68.5	82.8	100.0
1979	59.5	66.4	81.1	100.0

* In percentages of the wage level of plants with 500 or more workers.

It is only natural for an imbalance to exist between wage levels in large enterprises and those in small ones, as is shown in Table 20 for the manufacturing industry. We see that from 1955 to 1965 the difference decreased. This was particularly true for workers in small plants employing less than 30 people: while their wages in 1960 were less than half those paid by plants with 500 or more, they rose to over 60 percent of the latter by 1965. Wages in plants with 30 to 99 workers also rose from just under 60 to 70 percent of those in the big plants. During the years from 1965 to 1979, however, this decrease in wage differences began to slow down. Small plants with less than 100 employees and very small plants followed the trend toward higher wages for the first twenty years after the beginning of economic growth, but had to limit raises thereafter, and the relative level of their wages has dropped slightly in recent years.

The decrease in wage level differences was due to the strong demand for labor during the period of rapid growth, when the supply tended to be inadequate. But wage level differences made it more difficult for medium, small and very small enterprises to obtain labor. At the present time there is almost no difference in starting wages at manufacturing plants, regardless of size. Nevertheless, small plants have difficulty attracting young workers, and they employ a smaller proportion than the large plants; on the other hand, they have a considerably higher proportion of middle-aged and old workers. For example, according to a survey by the Ministry of Labor on the age structure of full-time workers in manufacturing industry, 58 percent of workers in small enterprises with 10–99 employees in 1958 were under 30, compared with 41 percent in large enterprises with more than 1,000 employees. In 1975 the percentages were 28 percent in the former and 38 percent in the latter. In contrast, in large enterprises fifteen years ago 28 percent were 40 years or older and now 29 percent are in this age group, while in the same period the percentage rose sharply from 23 to 43 percent in small enterprises. This shows a remarkable rise in the average age of employees in small enterprises.

As to sexual differentiation among workers, during the period of rapid growth the number of working women steadily increased. In 1971 there was for the first time a slight decrease from the previous year. Although it showed an increase in 1973, the number has had a tendency to decrease in these years of depression. At present women constitute 35 percent of the total employed population. Although they constitute a large proportion of Japan's labor force, on the whole there are great differences between female and male workers. Women are strongly affected by the strain of coping with both domestic and career demands. As of 1978 the average length of employment for men was 10.8 years, while that for women was about half of men's, 6 years; even allowing for this factor, the average wage for women is only 56 percent of that of men. Figures for 1975 show that 32.4 percent of females continue their education past the high school level (including 5.7 percent for junior colleges), as compared with 44.1 percent for males (including 3.7 percent for junior colleges). These percentages suggest that the question of female employment will be an important issue in the future. Employment opportunities for women must be expanded, and job conditions should be the same as those for men. A way must be found to make women's work and home life compatible. Women must be given the opportunity to return to a job after their children are older.

The Japanese employment situation contains discriminatory practices among enterprises and between the sexes. It will be difficult to reduce wage discrepancies and the differences in health and welfare benefits a company provides, which all vary depending on company size. Although the dual economic structure is being modified, it continues to dominate certain aspects of the economy; to some extent its contradictions are becoming greater. As a result, it is difficult to achieve solidarity among workers even when they work in the same industry. Other differences in their situation stem from the need for workers in tiny paternalistic enterprises to struggle simply for survival, while some workers in large enterprises have become politically apathetic, since their companies and positions are economically secure.

3. Management and Labor Unions

Generally speaking, paternalistic management has been a characteristic of Japanese enterprise from the outset. At first labor in most entrepreneurial endeavors lacked stability, but gradually the principle of lifelong employment and a wage system based on seniority were adopted. Worker loyalty to a paternalistic management was reinforced by various kinds of welfare facilities and services granted as fringe benefits in addition to cash wages.

This tradition survived the war. It was tempered to incorporate such postwar changes, however, as the growth of labor unions. To rationalize management, it was necessary to give recognition to ability and adopt a pay system based on the level of service performed and one's function in the company. Labor-management relations also have changed. Such procedures as labor-management conferences and labor participation in management, inconceivable before the war, have been adopted along with employee suggestion programs and methods to air grievances. American experiments in on-the-job training have also been introduced.

Paternalistic management has not been replaced, however much it may have been criticized, and the recent growth of Japanese enterprises seems to have strengthened its grip. Company unions have opposed modification of the seniority wage system, but it has changed, nonetheless, so as to reflect more fairly an employee's function and the nature of his job. The mobility of labor today is high enough to undercut the power of the "lifelong employment" system; the latter continues in force, however, and efforts are still made to ensure the loyalty of the worker to his company. This is facilitated, as we shall see later, by the fact that labor unions are organized on an enterprise basis.

To counteract labor unions, management has organized the Japan Federation of Employers' Associations (*Nihon Keieisha Renmei — Nikkeiren*), and has also set up the Federation of Economic Organizations (*Keizai Dantai Rengōkai — Keidanren*), which represents the interests of the entire business community on various political and economic matters. These organizations, although different in nature, act in harmony to protect and make even more secure the position of management.

Meanwhile, workers have built up their own extensive organization of labor unions since the war. In 1935 the number of workers in unions was a mere 410,000, not quite 7 percent of all employed workers. In 1946, right after the Labor Union Law went into effect as part of the wave of "democratization," 3.75 million or 40 percent of all employed workers were organized into unions. Thereafter the unions expanded very rapidly. In 1948–49 the number of union members exceeded 4.6 million, and the percentage of organized labor stood at 56 percent.

Unions then entered into a period of retrenchment. In 1950 the percentage of unionized workers dropped by 10 percent. This percentage has continued to decrease despite a gradual increase in the number of union members. In 1950 there were 5.8 million union members; at present there are nearly 12.4 million, but the percentage of organized labor is only 30.8 percent. Between 1960 and 1975 the number of individual unions increased from about 40,000 to 72,000; as manufacturing, commerce and the service industries grew, however, those organized into unions were proportionately fewer, despite higher employment rates. Unions have been organized in almost all the large enterprises, but many small and tiny enterprises have none. In sum, union organization is not keeping pace with the increase in the number of workers.

Most unions are organized in a way characteristic to Japan; that is, by individual enterprise, and embracing blue-collar and white-collar, factory and office workers in the same union. This kind of plant-by-plant union organization fits the paternalistic idea of enterprise as one big family. The workers, too, see no contradiction in being loyal to both their company and their union—a fact that constitutes a built-in limitation on union effectiveness.

Each local union is ordinarily affiliated with a national industrial union, which is, in turn, a member of a national center. The Japan Council of Industrial Organizations (*Zennihon Sangyōbetsu Rōdō Kumiai Kaigi*—abbreviated, *Sanbetsu*) was the most powerful national center until shortly after the war, when it was dissolved and reorganized. After 1950 hegemony was transferred to the General Council of Japanese Labor Unions (*Nihon Rōdō Kumiai Sōhyōgikai*—*Sōhyō*: 4.55 million), but the national labor front as a whole has been further split into the Japanese Confederation of Labor (*Zennihon Rōdō Sōdōmei*—*Dōmei*: 2.16 million), the Federation of Independent Unions (*Chūritsu Rōdō Kumiai Renraku Kaigi*— *Chūritsu Rōren*: 1.36 million), and the National Federation of Industrial Organizations (*Zennihon Sangyōbetsu Rōdō Kumiai Rengōkai*— *Shinsanbetsu*: 62,000). A movement is developing to reorganize and unite the labor front, but the direction it will take is yet to be seen.

While the number of labor disputes and those involved in them have been increasing, the past ten years or so have focused on annual wage hikes gained in the "spring offensive." Serious strikes and go-slow campaigns have been confined mainly to small enterprises. Because these tactics have been successful so far and working conditions have improved, the labor situation is presently relatively placid, and the unions cannot move a largely political membership to action. Union leaders have gained considerable negotiating and bargaining skills, and leaders of national labor organizations look to politics as the means to further progress. As a result the reformist parties have become all the more dependent on the unions. Under these circumstances, the labor unions lack the power to overcome the long-lasting political power .of the conservative governing party. While management is able to act in a coherent, unified way, the top labor union organizations are limited by their own particular ideological positions and weakened by their inability to take united action.

To the extent that individual unions are formed on an enterprise basis, their members and leaders are accustomed to looking at issues from a corporate point of view, and they are extremely conservative in regard to their own vested interests. To cite one example, the health insurance programs of small enterprises are under government management and are very unfavorable compared with those organized for employees of large corporations; yet the labor unions are reluctant to push for reform. They feel that they benefit by being able to use the surplus funds from their health insurance programs to build up welfare facilities in their own enterprises.

The number of employees in the manufacturing industry is large but the proportion organized into unions is conspicuously lower than in mining, transportation and communications, and public service. In many industries such as commerce and services, very little progress is being made in unionizing medium and small enterprises. These unorganized workers may be assumed to be completely under paternalistic management, and because their level of social security is low they are all the more dependent on management. Efforts to bridge this gap between organized and unorganized labor are difficult to assess, but the difficulty is certainly compounded by a feeling of superiority on the part of workers securely employed in large corporations in regard to the unorganized workers of medium and small enterprises. They seem to have no desire for the unity and solidarity of labor as a whole; furthermore, regardless of their vocal support for labor-farmer cooperation, they have done practically nothing to promote that cause. As long as the present situation persists wherein each enterprise union gives priority to its own interests, organized labor will not become the principal factor in Japanese politics.

Frustrated at the lack of action, extremists have arisen among young dissatisfied workers influenced by antiwar, left-wing groups. The changing attitude of labor and the widening generation gap necessitate some serious reflection on what the future of labor unions should be.

4. Labor and Technological Innovation

Labor in a capitalist society can be considered "forced" labor, in the sense that it constitutes the sale of manpower for wages, binding the laborer during his working hours. During the feudal period the independent artisan had his own means of production and performed his work in his own home. He could find lasting satisfaction in the pleasure of turning out a finished product. The modern worker has lost the means of production and commutes to a factory where he works for a fixed period under a system of division of labor. It is generally hard for him to find satisfaction in life. If he is interested in his work and finds it pleasant, this is usually not because of the work itself but because of the good income it brings or the prestige he gains from it. Even then, he is bound to have some feeling of alienation—of being left out.

In modern society labor has become more and more mechanized, specialized, and rationalized. The production process is broken down into tiny segments, simple tasks are repeated over and over again to the tempo of the machine. Labor merely becomes a means of earning the wages to satisfy one's needs. The worker who must faithfully handle his share of the production flow as it comes to him on a conveyor belt becomes nothing more than a cog in the machinery. This typical worker in the machine age forfeits his own individuality as long as he is working at his job.

Recent technical innovations have increased mechanization of the work in large industrial plants. In heavy industry, machines are being introduced to displace laborers, forcing them to subordinate their movements to the movements of these machines. Furthermore, there has been great progress in automation, with the petroleum-refining industry leading the way. Manual labor has diminished, but instead workers are forced into the monotonous work of overseeing the operation of the automated processes. At a job where he cannot take his eyes off gauges and meters for an instant, where he is isolated from normal human relations, the worker undergoes greater mental than physical fatigue.

The introduction of computers and the high rate of conversion to automation has forced this kind of labor into an increasingly rationalized mold. According to one view, application of technological advances would seem to require a high degree of knowledge and training, thus promoting the development of specialization. The number of technical specialists who actually run an automated factory, however, is extremely small compared with the great number of workers who, subordinated to the machines, perform simple repetitive operations or mere monitoring of the operation of the machines. These masses of workers can come close to losing their identities as human beings. Even in their own labor union these workers end up as lone figures caught in a huge net of bureaucracy. They cannot expect to maintain their human identities at their places of work.

Such a worker has to seek recovery outside his work. In his own home he can find release from his feeling of isolation at work. Perhaps he may recover his personal identity in the pursuit of pleasure or in gambling. The hours of work per week in Japan's manufacturing industry are still longer than those in other advanced countries, even though by 1979 they had been reduced to 41.1 hours, by just seven hours from the 1960 average of 48.1. The five-day week, which was introduced in about 1970, is gradually spreading, especially in large corporations. As of 1978, 33 percent of businesses with 1,000 or more employees (6 percent of the total number) gave two full days off a week; if we include those which give two days off every other week, the proportion is 88 percent (45 percent of the total). Improvements in working conditions will liberate the workers to a certain extent from the isolation they feel while on the job. But if improvements go no further than giving them more hours of escape in the refuge of their homes or providing opportunities to compensate for the frustrations of their working conditions by leisure-time pleasures, the problem of personal identity on the job will not be solved.

Medium and small enterprises are also affected by technical innovation; the difference is only one of degree. In commerce, too, which is less susceptible to rationalization, working conditions are changing. There remains more latitude for independent action by the workers, as they are more difficult to organize, but growing control of operations by computers in large enterprises is pushing labor toward the pattern common in industrial plants. The same trend is increasing in government offices and in the business offices of companies. In this respect, the working conditions of white-collar and blue-collar workers are becoming more similar.

Many workers have become cogs in the big machine of the mass-production society, but those who work in tiny enterprises and day laborers who lack job security and a fixed place of employment remain outside that pattern. Their work still depends on manual labor, and because of its insecurity anxiety impels them to that cup of saké or to such diversions as gambling. Also not to be forgotten are the farm-family workers who take additional jobs in other occupations. Except for those who commute to regular jobs, their work is not steady, their earnings are low, and the additional work leads to excessive fatigue. This group constitutes an important and often problematic element in the labor force, particularly in the construction industry.

At the end of 1971 a survey of workers' attitudes toward their lives was made by the Ministry of Labor. With regard to general satisfaction with their life—both at work and at home—3 percent expressed themselves as fairly well satisfied; 37 percent as just barely satisfied; 12 percent were greatly dissatisfied; and 41 percent were rather dissatisfied. This survey shows a strong tendency toward overall dissatisfaction with their work. Workers are seeking (with little success) "work that is meaningful and worthwhile." Table 21 is taken from a survey by the National Livelihood Research Center. In 1962, according to the survey, 26 percent of the respondents considered work a duty or a pleasure, while in 1970 the proportion was not quite 20 percent. Those who made a distinction between the two ("work is work; play is play") and

Table 21. Changes in Attitudes toward Work (%)

	1962	1970
Because work is a man's duty, I work as much as I have time for.	16.2	11.0
Work is a pleasure.	9.6	8.3
Work is work; play is play.	41.2	39.6
Work is a means of making a living.	6.7	4.6
I like work, but recreation, too, is necessary.	21.6	28.6
I want to do what I want when I want to.	1.6	4.4
Undecided, or no reply.	3.2	3.6

those who liked work but considered recreation also necessary increased from 63 percent to 68 percent. If we analyze this table further, we see a marked decrease in those who consider work a duty, and a clear increase in those who emphasize the importance of recreation. Moreover, while the percentage of those who want to do what they want when they want is still small, there has been a considerable increase in this sentiment. Results of later surveys by the Center are not shown in Table 21 since the questions themselves have been changed, but the 1976 survey results can be summarized as follows: seven percent of the respondents regarded their work as something to live for; those who enjoy their leisure life but put emphasis on their work amounted to 43 percent; those who took as much interest in leisure life as in their work, 30 percent; more interest in leisure life than in work, 11 percent; and those who exerted themselves only for leisure life, 4 percent. In a 1975 survey by the Prime Minister's Office, 46 percent of the respondents said they felt a sense of fulfilment when in the bosom of their families. This figure by far exceeded that of those who felt that they were most fulfilled when devoting themselves to their work, 33 percent. If we examine the responses to these questions by age groups, we find that the younger people are and the higher their level of education, the more dissatisfied they are with work, and that the younger they are, the more they seek to find a meaningful life in their spare time.

According to the Ministry of Labor survey and considering the overall averages, workers who feel that life is most worthwhile when they are devoted to their work and when they gain recognition from others by it amount to 37 percent. The 1974 survey by the Ministry of Labor showed that about 25 percent of workers consider that their capabilities are reflected in their work, regardless of the size of the enterprises they belong to and whether they are white- or blue-collar workers, with the only exception being that the percentage is a little higher among blue-collar workers in small enterprises. It is doubtful that they will continue to feel their work is worthwhile for the same reasons, since greater progress in technical innovations will probably intensify the feeling of alienation. In a society with such high productivity levels is it inevitable that only a small number of people can seek a meaningful, worthwhile life in their work, while the great majority must try to find such satisfaction in their leisure time by means of higher wages? If it is acceptable to seek happiness outside work through increased earnings the rise in earnings will produce spiraling personal demands and hopeless work alienation. It will then be difficult to do anything about trying to educate people on the issue of discriminatory differences in earnings. Until the worker can feel that work is not just a means of acquiring money to make life pleasant but is a useful contribution to society, he cannot come to experience a really worthwhile life. So long as he is unable to lead a life that is substantial and personally worthwhile, his feeling of alienation will probably continue, and his attempts to escape it will give rise to even greater distortions in society.

VI. Mass Society and Mass Culture

1. Developing Mass Society

Modern society evolves out of the disintegration of the tight-knit communal society of village and town. As production under a capitalist system develops, men leave towns and villages to work in factories. Not possessing the means of production, they must sell their labor. The development of transportation and communication leads to greater expansion of markets and the formation of commercial centers—the city.

However, during the early stage of development of a capitalist economy in modern society, many independent farmers and proprietors remain in the towns and villages. These towns and villages still form an important proportion of the total society, thereby maintaining the traditional stability of the social order. Japan was in this stage throughout the Meiji period.

As the economy enters the stage of monopoly capitalism, an increasing number of people are cut off from the close-knit society of the village. The old middle class begins to break up and the proportion of the new middle class and worker class rises. As the new middle class expands to embrace a sizable part of the population and more and more workers are employed in large factories, both white- and blue-collar classes emerge as a mass severed from the traditional communities. This group is the seedbed for a transition to mass society. In Japan the initial movement toward mass society occurred during the 1920s, between the "Taishō democracy" period and the advent of Japanese fascism.

Japan's mass society attained full-scale development during the period of growth after the war. A mass society is characterized by a highly advanced economy and high mass consumption. As we have already seen, the white-collar and blue-collar classes increased tremendously, with a corresponding decrease in the number of independent proprietors and family workers. Moreover, the differences between white-collar and blue-collar workers have decreased since the end of the war. Neither have prospects of long-term social security, for one thing, but both have sufficient income to support large-scale consumption in a highly industrialized society.

At work this mass of people is involved in only a small sector of the total business and production process and plays only a passive role in the bureaucratized trade unions. The personal relationships one finds in the village cannot exist in this thoroughly rationalized society; hence, contacts with others are impersonal, marked by lack of intimacy and a sense of isolation. Reduced to mere atoms in a giant social mechanism, people experience a feeling of helplessness. Even though everyone else in this mass society is similarly cut off from small communal society, there are no bonds to tie everyone together; all have different origins, occupations and social classes. Their educational backgrounds and upbringing are also varied. With no community to ease the feelings of isolation and helplessness and no common traditions or customs, they live in a kind of anomie. The hustle and bustle and congestion of the large cities are necessary, often welcome, appendages to the lives of these people, but having committed themselves to this crowded existence, they remain lonely for lack of human contacts. Constituents of a mass society end up becoming an anonymous majority, an amorphous crowd.

The only place for them to turn to is their families. "My-home-ism"—the introspective tendency to withdraw into one's own family—is a logical development in mass society. But the family cannot always be an adequate refuge from feelings of isolation and helplessness. When a man finally does not find security in his family life, he may seek escape in nationalism, or worse, he may be lured by the appeal of fascism.

Their jobs make these people mere cogs in the machine or so many scattered grains of sand. As a result they are constantly frustrated. Unsatisfied desires can at a certain point lead to severe emotional outbursts. Herein may lie the irrationality of the usual mob. At the end of the last century Gustave Le Bon spoke critically, of mass democracy as the rule of the crowd. Gabriel Tarde, however, claimed that the essence of democracy itself rested in the public, and he trusted they would assume that responsibility. Le Bon's attitude derives from a contempt for the masses and mistakenly underestimates their creative energy. However, in the development of a mass society, an image of the masses as an emotional, irrational crowd is more likely to result than the image of a logical, rational group of citizens acting in the interest of the public good.

People lived in the communal society of premodern villages and towns as the "tradition-directed" men in the sense formulated by David Riesman. Such people merely followed tradition and customs handed down from ancient times. Japanese society continued to produce that type of individual for a long time, well after the Meiji Restoration. It did not encourage patterns of individual development that would lead to what Riesman calls the "inner-directed" man. The "tradition-directed" Japanese had few resources to make personal decisions when confronted with the kind of external change that modernization brought with it; as the world around him took on the characteristics of mass society, his reaction was to conform. In the process, he learned to go along with authority and prevailing trends; he became "other-directed."

The peculiar pattern of Japan's mass society is most conspicuous in densely populated urban areas, where the new middle and the working classes have increased most rapidly. The characteristics of mass society are now spreading to many sectors of the population. Urban expansion is accelerating this trend, but in rural villages and older downtown shopping districts the communal social structures are breaking up. Most farm families have jobs in addition to farming, and city families with small enterprises also work as employees elsewhere, just to make a living. This trend to do additional work has given further impetus to the spread of conditions of mass society.

Communication and the media have naturally undergone tremendous change since the war. The mass media have exerted pressure that has driven consumption to new heights, while cajoling the citizen to frantically seek recreation facilities and more free time. The result is a surging "leisure boom," a mass race to have as much "fun" as the next fellow.

2. Mass Communication

Rapid expansion of communication facilities is a basic condition for the growth of a society. Mass media developed most rapidly after the war. Until 1920 newspapers and magazines were the primary media, but they were soon outstripped. Radio broadcasting began in 1925, television broadcasting in 1953, and color television in 1967. TV has by now become the main medium of mass communication.

When television was introduced, the Japanese economy was still in the recovery stage and only limited numbers of people could afford the highly priced sets. In 1960 there were only 23.1 registered sets per 100 households, but by 1967 this figure rose to 79.8, and in 1970 to 81.9. Registration has stayed at that level thereafter; but at present over 98 percent of households have color television sets, so that telecasts reach almost every household. Television has become inseparable from modern life and has come to exert a strong influence on those who watch it daily. According to a National Broadcasting Corporation (NHK) survey, about 90 percent of the population watch television. They watch it an average of three hours and thirty minutes on weekdays, one-half more than the time spent in other advanced countries. Unlike radio, to which one can listen while doing something else, television demands constant attention of the viewer. This, in a sense, has changed the time structure of everyday life. Television has also resulted in a decline in the motion picture industry. Until about 1960 popular films still sold 3.5 admission tickets per capita annually, but this dropped to 2.5 in 1970, and has since declined to less than 1.5. In the same period, the total number of movie theaters in the country decreased from 4,300 to 2,400.

As television spread, the relative importance of radio declined. Radio has not become obsolete, however; small portable radios and car radios still occupy an important position in the communications media. For example, active efforts are made to stimulate an exchange between radio listeners and broadcasters (in contrast to television's essentially passive activity), and this has somewhat reversed the decline of radio. Late-night broadcasts attract younger listeners in particular.

Newspapers held a monopoly in mass communications from the beginning of the modern era until very recently, but they have lost ground to the broadcasting media. Despite this fact, they are still bought and read by many people. The circulation of the daily newspapers amounts to over 560 per thousand persons, thus putting Japan in competition for first place among the countries of the world.

Japanese newspapers are not distinguished by class of readership. The five national papers, the three major regional newspapers, and the prefectural newspapers are all very much alike. Over half of the total copies published in Japan are the national and regional newspapers. Most are delivered to residences through newspaper distribution agencies. Except for the political party organs, the dailies claim to be politically neutral, and, as we shall see later, their dependence on advertising tends to impose indirect restrictions on what they publish.

A few large newspaper companies have established what amounts to hierarchies of control over other media by means of ownership of and affiliation with a great many subsidiary or related companies. These include local and other broadcasting companies. Consequently, these newspapers have achieved a position of dominant control over much of the mass media. The large newspaper companies also publish weekly magazines and sports tabloids, either on their own or through their subsidiary companies, thus maintaining a firm grip on the greater part of Japan's mass communications media.

Before the war weekly magazines were published by only two or three large newspaper companies; later, magazine publishers entered the field and, since 1956, the number and variety of periodicals has increased tremendously. Weeklies have surpassed monthly magazines not only in circulation but also as an important medium of mass communications. They contain miscellaneous short articles catering to popular tastes and can be thrown away upon being read; this is one factor contributing to the stagnation of the older book publishing industry. Japan ranks after the Soviet Union, America, West Germany and Great Britain in number of books published. However, while the number of new publications is increasing, the number of books being reprinted is decreasing.

Japan's communications media have had a huge impact on modernization and the growth of industrial society. The advent of television, however, sounded a warning that this new machine would make Japan a nation of a hundred million idiots. The media can disseminate a vast amount of information, and the effect on those who receive it may be to create a people with standardized tastes, behavior and thinking. Thus, if most people watch and listen to low-level programs with little intellectual or moral value, we may be encouraging a mass degeneration of intellectual interest and capacity. If on the other hand, the mass media can inspire new aspirations and positively influence the values and standards of thinking, they will assist in the transition to a modern and humane society. The potential to learn is strong in every viewer. However, if commercial programs exploit the human interest in vulgar amusement and sensationalism, they are performing a great disservice to the people. The tendency to aim programs at the lowest level of enjoyment weakens the critical faculties of viewers and listeners and results in a move toward conformity. When watching television becomes a temporary escape from reality, then this medium becomes merely an opiate and cannot be an uplifting force in any mass culture.

Today, daily newspapers cannot compete with television news in speed of reporting; by the time he gets his paper the reader has been informed of the important news, so he skips the lead articles and reads other sections, for example the sports pages. The sports tabloids, which also supply much news concerning mass amusements, are widely read for their specialist treatment. While many professional baseball players are well known, a great many people probably cannot recall the names of today's cabinet ministers. Today people are avidly interested in TV personalities, and weekly magazines carrying articles on their private lives sell extraordinarily well. A story about the marital difficulties of a famous star attracts more interest than something such as a crucial remark dropped by a cabinet minister. Ultimately, the mass media foster political apathy, thus multiplying the negative aspects of mass society.

A major reason why the mass media, particularly television, have an overall negative influence on society is that they have become essentially advertising media. Newspapers are dependent more on advertising than on subscriptions for their revenue, the ratio being about 6 to 4. With the exception of NHK, broadcasting companies are almost totally supported by their sponsors. Mass consumption has led to more advertising. As shown in Table 22, newspapers' share in paid advertising, which twenty-five years ago was over half, has dropped, while television has absorbed one-third of the total. Television commercials have increased mass consumption also. Since those who pay for the advertising expect results, the percentage of viewers a station commands becomes an important standard. Advertising consequently becomes sensational and programs grow more vulgar in order to attract a greater number of viewers.

Table 22. Breakdown of Advertising Expenditures by Medium (%)

	Newspapers	Magazines	Radio	Television	Other
1955	55.3	5.7	16.1	1.5	21.4
1965	35.8	5.6	4.7	32.2	21.7
1975	33.1	5.4	4.8	34.0	22.7
1980	31.1	5.6	5.2	34.6	23.5

3. Consumption and Popular Attitudes toward Life

Japan's fast-growing economy has greatly changed consumer patterns in daily life. Before the war Japanese regarded consumer buying as a kind of vice; now, while not exactly a virtue, high consumer spending is acceptable, or even prestigious. The low level of social security continues to encourage the Japanese to save and be frugal, but advanced marketing techniques have stimulated a tendency to spend more on consumer goods, a tendency that as a whole has risen. Especially striking has been the rise of consumer spending in rural villages; the aura of high-level mass consumption has enveloped them, too, as it spreads throughout the country.

Table 23.   The Rise in Level of Consumption (1965 = 100)

	Nationwide	Urban	Rural
1960	77.4	78.9	72.8
1965	100.0	100.0	100.0
1970	131.8	126.7	146.9
1975	155.8	143.8	194.1
1979	168.9	154.7	216.0

After the war mass consumption dropped steeply to about half that of the late twenties and early thirties. A shortage of food and the struggle just to eat forced urban residents in particular to sell and barter their family goods for food. Ten years later the level of consumption was restored to its prewar level, and thereafter it rose rapidly. The Engel coefficient, which in about 1935 was 50 for farm families and 36 for city workers, stood at about 40 for both around 1960. Today it has dropped to 29 for city workers and 24 for farm families.

Along with a decreasing Engel coefficient, consumption rose to new high levels between 1955 and 1960. The economy reached a peak in 1956–58, called the "Jimmu boom," when it surpassed prewar levels. As already stated, television sets, washing machines and refrigerators were bought widely at that time and were dubbed the "Three Sacred Treasures." They were soon taken for granted as household necessities by the average person, whose style of life was being Westernized; eating habits, household furnishings and clothing all changed. In recent years the car, color TV and air conditioner, known as the "three C's," became items sought by all families. Ownership of consumer durables has risen so rapidly in such a short period of time that twenty years ago no one could have imagined that by the early 1980s about 60 percent of Japan's households would own a car.

Table 24. Ownership of Principal Durable Consumer Goods (%)

	Electric washing machine	Refrig- erators	Black & white TV	Vacuum cleaner	Camera	Color TV	Car
1960	40.6	10.1	44.7	7.7	45.8	—	—
1965	68.5	51.4	90.0	32.2	49.4	—	9.1
1970	91.4	89.1	90.2	68.3	64.1	26.3	22.1
1975	97.6	96.1	48.7	92.7	77.4	90.3	41.2
1980	98.8	99.1	22.8	95.8	82.9	98.2	57.2

In addition to consumer durables, expenditures for leisure activities have been rising. The yearly increase in earnings has been accompanied by less time spent at work or household tasks. Watching television or napping during leisure time is still common, but in recent years people have begun more active leisure pursuits. Traveling or going for drives has become very common. According to a 1970 survey, the percentages of households taking trips with overnight stays of one or more nights were 30 percent during the spring, 46 percent during the summer, and 33 percent during the autumn. The main form of such travel is shifting from group excursions to individual and family trips. Over half of the summer trips made were by families traveling together. With 1970 as the peak, sightseeing recreation decreased slightly and has remained on the same level. In 1975, for example, 72 people out of one hundred took short trips, assuming one trip for each. In the meantime one-day trips amounted to about four times the number of short trips in the same year. Moreover, we have to note that the number of those who have made overseas trips increased from 660,000 to 4 million between 1970 and 1980.

Feelings about the way one lives have also changed greatly. We touched on attitudes of workers in the preceding chapter, and we saw that they once considered recreation as free time literally to "recreate" their vitality in order to work. Now one might say that work is performed for the sake of leisure. The *homo ludens* type of man who considers consumer spending, amusement and pleasure the goals of life has become surprisingly numerous. According to surveys by the Prime Minister's Office in 1960, 45 percent of the population considered themselves as middle-middle class or above. In 1976 this rose to 69 percent, a substantial increase brought about mainly by the rise in the level of consumption. The same attitude in turn causes that level to rise further, and strengthens the trend toward pleasure in leisure time. Asked to choose between more money and more leisure, most respondents in a late 1960s survey by the Prime Minister's Office chose increased income even if it meant longer working hours, but in the 1972 survey the majority chose shorter working hours over increased income. According to the 1975 survey, those who said they preferred increased income exceeded those who chose short working hours: however, this does not necessarily mean that the trend was reversed again, since the largest portion of the respondents were accounted for by those who could not clearly say which they would prefer. The result was probably due to the fact that people have been more or less successful in their pursuit of leisure while their real income has been stagnant for the past few years. Asked whether they seek life satisfaction in work or in the pleasures of life, many more chose the latter. A recent survey by the Ministry of Labor showed that less than 20 percent of the respondents sought life satisfaction in their work. Not a few in high-income brackets are inclined to seek satisfaction in their work, but for those with relatively low incomes, work becomes just a means to make pleasure available. These people, supported by rises in income, are spending increasing amounts of money on their leisure activities.

These changes in consumer patterns have been so rapid that they were bound to cause distortions in "ordinary" life styles. For example, we find people living in cramped public housing (two rooms and a dinette-kitchen) who own a car which they use only for Sunday driving, or the family in a private apartment house that occupies one six-mat (about 9' × 12') room crowded with furniture and appliances, in which there is scarcely space for everybody to sleep. Japan ranks with the leading countries of the world in the distribution of durable consumer goods, and yet the poverty of the material environment still remains. Although Japan now has one-tenth the residential assets of the U.S., and about one-third those of West Germany, there is no question that the living environment is sorely inadequate.

Most Japanese today, in spite of a steady rise in income, do not consider their lives very comfortable. The rise in the level of consumption has in many ways acted to limit the comfort of their lives. According to public opinion polls conducted each year by the Prime Minister's Office on popular attitudes toward living conditions, about 25 percent consider their lives more difficult than in the year before, while only about 10 percent say that their lives have improved. Seven out of ten respondents consider their present lives more or less satisfactory. Slightly fewer consider themselves as middle-middle class or higher. But as long as their frustrations are such that trips and drives must become palliatives, and as long as expenditures for these continue to increase, their lives can scarcely be said to be comfortable. It is inevitable that, as desires and expectations grow, people become more aware of the low level of government spending on public facilities that private spending can by no means provide. This tendency has become especially evident in the past several years.

4.   Mass Amusements and Gambling

Today, the home television set provides everyday amusement for almost everyone. But people have a great deal of free time, and even though they may spend nearly three and a half hours a day watching television, they do not rely on this for all their amusement. Sightseeing trips (whose popularity has resulted in a rapid growth in the tourist industry) and Sunday drives are a wholesome kind of amusement, but they cannot be engaged in every day. A great many divert themselves from frustrations by drinking in bars or at street stands, or by amusing themselves at professional baseball games, wrestling or boxing matches.

In another area, the striptease, which was extremely popular among men for a time after the war, declined, and Turkish baths —which have replaced the red-light district in some of their functions—sprang up in every city. When movie theaters lost much of their audiences to television, they began to attract more people by showing pornographic films. Furthermore, as a by-product of the motorcar culture, motels—commonly established for illicit rendezvous—are sprouting up along the highways.

Gambling is another form of mass amusement that can take such diverse forms as mahjong or *pachinko* (Japanese pinball), and bicycle, horse, boat or automobile races. Although gambling is illegal in mahjong clubs, this game nonetheless often involves some gambling. One can develop a compulsive enjoyment of mahjong that enables one to forget everything else and to feel satisfaction and superiority if one wins.

Pachinko used to be a game for the amusement of children and was found at recreation centers, but later it rapidly became a popular pastime for adults. Just after the end of the war people would crowd into *pachinko* halls, forget their troubles, and delight in selling the prizes they won. That *pachinko* has not lost popularity bespeaks the general insecurity that exists in spite of great economic growth. To follow the course of the little ball in a *pachinko* machine lets one temporarily escape from reality and satisfy some of the gambling spirit without having to spend much money.

As local municipal governments sought sources of revenue after the war, gambling at bicycle, boat and auto races was legalized and managed by the municipal bodies. Horse racing, which existed before the war, is somewhat different, but recently the number of people who buy parimutuel tickets has increased. All of these various race tracks are found throughout the country and attract large crowds. It seems that different social classes are attracted to different forms of legalized gambling, exhibiting a kind of social pathology. For example, the lower classes seem to habituate bicycle races, the most widespread of the races, while other groups bet on horses, etc.

The phenomenon of universal gambling in a mass society is not a problem unique to Japan, but a worldwide trend. It is an unwholesome development. Insecurity and uneasiness about life leads to gambling as a temporary escape and as excitement for the speculating mind.

A desire to escape and to forget one's troubles sometimes motivates avid interest in professional baseball and the sports papers. This is far more wholesome than gambling, and an increase in interest here is desirable in itself. Participant sports are even more beneficial than spectator sports, but there are not enough facilities for ordinary sports. Although golf courses are being built one after another, they are far too expensive for most. Athletic fields where the public can enjoy sports are extremely few. The popularity of golf has become widespread, and golfing circles are not limited to the upper classes. Still, it has not yet become a mass amusement, and the athletic value of the sport is undermined by its image as a status symbol. Those who play golf are often under the illusion that it will help them go up a step in the social ladder.

In any case recreation and leisure have come to be regarded as one of the goals of human life. Some say that the original meaning of the word "leisure" is the devotion of free time to "learning." Leisure should be used to raise the level of one's culture, increase one's interest in social and political matters and result in the kind of happiness that would turn people away from the pursuit of transitory amusements and make life really meaningful. Present prospects for better use of free time are not, however, very bright.

VII. Social Ills and Destruction of the Environment

1. Old and New Poverty

Although Japan was once very poor, its agricultural productivity has always been high compared with other Asian countries. For this reason it is the single Asian nation that has been able to achieve industrial development and growth of a capitalist economy with no outside assistance.

A policy aimed at increasing national wealth and military strength was the motivating force behind this development. Special favors and encouragements were given to industry, and higher productivity and large sums of money were invested in building a modern military force. The poverty that was left in the wake of Japan's spectacular national economic development was given scant attention, however. To most it was inevitable and therefore seemed hopeless—a necessary by-product of industrialization. The poverty of the urban lower classes was no less abject than the destitution of tenant farmers in the villages; nevertheless, with the exception of the rice riots following World War I, the poor in Japan never erupted in social outbreaks violent enough to force recognition of a basic social problem.

Measures for alleviating what had become an urgent problem were not taken. Within the very framework of Japanese society there existed devices for absorbing or ignoring poverty; there was a strong tendency, for instance, to regard poverty as a misfortune that one must simply become resigned to, and there was a lack of awareness of the social causes of poverty. The idea that society itself should be responsible for relieving that which it had caused never occurred to most. The Meiji government made a beginning in helping the poor with the establishment of the Relief Regulations in 1874; and in 1929 a national aid system, the Relief and Assistance Law, was adopted. But these measures fell far short of providing real relief. Also, the people had a deeply-rooted tendency to regard relief as shameful; poverty was something for the family and relatives to take care of themselves. Poverty which could not be handled in this way was considered a problem of unfortunates to be taken care of by charitable activities. Those who lacked even relatives to help them were simply pitied as the lowest of the unfortunate. The attitude that people had a right to assistance from society through a national welfare system simply did not exist.

After the war these attitudes underwent great change. At the end of 1945, when poverty was rampant, the general outlines of emergency relief for the needy were set up in a Cabinet meeting and the Daily Life Security Law went into effect. This law provided for national aid to the poor and needy on an equal basis without discrimination. The idea that it was a disgrace to become a "card-carrier," one who was entitled to government assistance, began to fade, and most began to take it for granted that those in need should receive help from government welfare policies. Relief from relatives, who now had no legal or even social obligation to help their cousins and nephews, decreased. Whereas before the war they would have been ashamed not to help, it was not long before they refused to help at all. Just after the war, nearly three million persons were receiving government assistance, 27 out of every 1,000. When Japan's economy entered its period of growth in 1955, these figures dropped to 1.7 or 1.8 million, or 20 out of every 1,000 and more recently, to 1.4 million, or 12 out of every 1,000. The increasing employment opportunities and rising wages that accompanied rapid economic growth have meant that many people have gone off relief. As a result, most families who now receive assistance are old people, mothers and children with no father, the mentally or physically handicapped, or the disabled. Such people make up almost 90 percent of the families on relief. In nearly 80 percent of those households no member is capable of working. It is especially noteworthy that while twenty years ago the head of the household was working in over 50 percent of families receiving relief, this ratio has now dropped to about 15 percent.

These statistics indicate that while poverty as such is decreasing, it is becoming more and more necessary for the aged, the mentally or physically handicapped and the disabled to be given long-term assistance. Assistance has increased steadily year after year, but the richer society as a whole becomes, the more keenly people feel their own poverty. This applies not only to those receiving public assistance but also to those whose economic level brings them down to the so-called borderline stratum. As part of a society that is growing increasingly more affluent, these people are painfully aware of their poverty. In this country the low-income strata that embrace these groups are estimated to be over 20 percent of the population.

Thus, modern Japanese society has not eliminated its old poverty; indeed, its huge economic growth is responsible for having created a new kind of poverty. Mixed in with the "old poor"— those on relief and others only a shade better off—are the "new poor," for whom their condition is all the more painful in an age of affluence and high mass consumption. New burdens on those left out of Japan's prosperity have been added to the old—psychological burdens. The prewar attitude of resignation to one's lot and of an unconcern for human rights is no longer possible, so, though the poor remain poor, it is more difficult for them to accept their lot.

In addition to poverty in the conventional sense of the word, Japanese society is becoming increasingly poor in a spiritual sense; although materially rich, something is lacking in the quality of life. Commercialized mass culture, hedonistic in its pursuit of pleasure, demonstrates a kind of cultural Gresham's law. Compared with "high-quality culture" there is no denying that the energy of Japan's masses is not developing to the fullest but is being degraded for commercial ends. Mass amusements such as those described earlier, which provide an outlet for sexual desire, and gambling, which becomes an escape from reality, only increase spiritual poverty; even among the materially affluent, crime and delinquency start to increase.

In addition, extraordinarily rapid economic growth is destroying the natural environment itself. What was once a rich, verdant nature is becoming an impoverished nature. This is causing a deterioration of the essential quality of human life. In the face of such jeopardy to the natural environment, we are beginning to realize that human life should be valued above all else. How long will it take for the idea of the ultimate worth of man to become embodied in social policy?

2. Those Left Behind

Before the war the physically or mentally handicapped, orphans and solitary old people without relatives managed to sustain themselves either through the help of relatives or by receiving charity from their localities. The few who had no relatives and could not support themselves by any means received aid from private social agencies. Public aid facilities were scanty, and most agencies of social work such as the charitable undertakings of religious organizations or of philanthropists could just barely struggle along.

This situation improved considerably after the war, and at present social welfare work is based on the Five Social Welfare Laws. This is the general name for individual welfare laws enacted for children, the aged, the physically handicapped, the mentally retarded, and mothers with children who are without the support of a father. The fact that relief and aid are now provided by law is a great change from the prewar situation, even though welfare facilities and personnel remain inadequate. Of the five laws, those for child welfare and for the physically handicapped were enacted soon after the war, in 1947 and 1949, respectively. Legislative measures for the mentally retarded, for the aged and for fatherless families were effected fairly recently, in 1960, 1963 and 1964, respectively.

The unfortunate people for whom these laws are designed are apt to be left behind in the surge of economic growth. Their voice in society is weak, legal measures to provide for them have lagged, and public welfare expenditures have not been given enough weight in the national budget. The first order of business in the government is growth in the economy. Social welfare work has, nonetheless, made great strides since the end of the war. The establishment of welfare offices in prefectures and cities has become obligatory, and 1,150 offices are now in operation. They are short of personnel, however; their activities are directed mainly toward assuring subsistence for the poor, and they do not get around to many other aspects of social welfare work. Though the number of caseworkers has recently gone up they are still too few. In the present situation subsidies for personnel expenditures are so small that agencies depend on the cooperation of social welfare councils. These are established on three levels: national; prefectural; and city, ward, town and village. Broadly classified, social welfare facilities may be divided into those for the care of the needy, welfare for the aged, rehabilitation of and assistance to the physically handicapped, protection of women, children's welfare, aid to the mentally retarded, mothers' welfare, etc. A more detailed classification would include fifty different kinds of facilities. The total number of such facilities at present is about 38,500, but 21,000 of them are day nurseries. Since two-thirds of the total number are public facilities and one-third private, in general the proportion of private social work is the reverse of what it was before the war.

The organization of social work is expanding, and the number of facilities has sharply increased in recent years, but the work as a whole is still inadequate. Compared with the striking rise in the standard of living of the population as a whole, the misery of uncared-for physically or mentally handicapped children and fatherless families has worsened. The increase in the proportion of the aged in the total population and the trend toward nuclear families have resulted in more and more elderly people who require social welfare. Physically and mentally these people have been excluded from the modern economy and society. It is no exaggeration to say that changes in methods of production and new applications of technology had the effect of depressing still further the lives of the handicapped and retarded. It is only recently that efforts have been made to promote social welfare corresponding to economic growth.

Although facilities are being built and becoming well equipped, there are not enough to accommodate those who need institutional care. Even if they are admitted to an institution it is likely to be short of personnel, so that they cannot get the kind of attention they need. For example, there was only one nursing home for the aged in 1963, when the Welfare Act for the Aged was enacted. Nursing homes for the aged have been expanding rapidly; in 1970, the number went over 150, and in 1978 it grew to 790 with total accommodations for 61,500 people. However, taking into consideration that there are about 350,000 aged people who need such care, and even after deducting from this number those who can rely on families at their own homes, present accommodating capacity is nowhere near enough. Moreover, institutions for children who are seriously handicapped mentally or physically can accommodate only about 30 percent of the total, and the number of institutions for severely mentally retarded and physically handicapped people comes nowhere near meeting the need, for they can accommodate only about 15 percent of those who should be admitted.

These institutions should always be staffed with trained, competent personnel, but people are more eager to select jobs that have better remuneration and working conditions. Japan is backward both in raising the level of institutes for specialist technical training and in providing salary scales appropriate to these specialities. The pay, working conditions and benefits in private institutions are well below the level in public ones. Strenuous efforts are urgently needed to raise salaries according to the work performed. If the people who take care of the needy are themselves left behind in the upward surge of the economy, there will be no light for future social welfare work in Japan.

It is not only the elderly, the orphaned, and the handicapped who have been left behind. Day laborers with irregular employment have been part of Japanese society since the beginning of industrial society. Although their numbers have decreased with the development of industry, many are still without the security of daily jobs, many cannot marry and support a family, and many have failed completely in trying to establish themselves in a job. The rapid growth of the economy has greatly expanded opportunities for employment, but it is difficult for the old or middle-aged man to change his occupation. Some were unable to shift from farming or coal mining, and in the course of long periods of working at jobs away from home they turned to casual labor. Many such people settle in the slums of the large cities; Tokyo's Sanya district and Osaka's Kamagasaki district are examples of such settlements. The very fact that these cheap lodging-house districts still exist illustrates one serious imbalance in Japanese society.

This group has been alienated, and rebellion against alienation sometimes leads to unhealthy mob riots. Outbursts at bicycle races (even though the fans are not necessarily slum-dwellers) are also rebellions against alienation by people who feel constantly frustrated. Such pathological social phenomena may occur at other places as well. Latent hostility has built up in those left behind by the economy; these people are on the lowest rung of a society which appears wealthy. The more wealthy the society, the more explosive this group is likely to become.

3. Crime and Delinquency

Crime and delinquency are the clearest manifestations of a socially pathological condition. Throughout the advanced world, these symptoms increase as income level rises. Crimes and misdemeanors can only be counted if they are first detected and prosecuted. Crimes that are never detected cannot become part of general statistics. In order to look at the trends and transitions in this area we need at least police statistics. According to these statistics, the total number of crimes by adults reached a peak in 1950, decreased thereafter, and have recently been on the rise again. Juvenile crimes followed the same pattern. In adult crime there has been an abrupt increase in cases of involuntary homicide and personal injury due to automobile accidents; the improvement in social and economic conditions has, on the other hand, been accompanied by only a slight decrease, or no change at all, in the amount of ordinary crime. The incidence of juvenile crime is rising rapidly. Exclusive of involuntary homicide and injury, about 40 percent of total arrestes are of juveniles. Taking into account the proportion of youths in the population, juvenile crime occurs five times more often than that of adults. This increase is striking, considering that twenty years ago it was about the same as that of adults.

When we examine crimes in 1979 (other than involuntary homicide due to occupational causes), 85 percent were those against
property, mainly theft, while assault, personal injury, intimidation
and extortion, murder, burglary, rape and arson accounted for
about 5 percent. Comparing this with the 1965 data, where the
former accounted for half of the total and the latter over 30 percent,
one can say that crimes against property have increased and crimes
of brutality have decreased. In particular, the latter declined by
one half during the seventies. There is a great deal of variation
between cities and rural areas in the incidence of crime, but urban
crime tends to be similar regardless of size of city. In general,
urbanization is causing diffusion of crime throughout the nation.
The ratio of crimes committed by people with steady jobs and no
previous criminal records is increasing, and crimes connected
with traffic accidents have soared with greater motorization.
Use of automobiles as an instrument of crime has become more
widespread.

These trends may be a reflection of changes and growth in the
economy, but the pattern here of a stagnant crime rate stands
in contrast to other advanced countries, where there is a direct
correlation between rise in incomes and in the crime rate. Perhaps
Japan is experiencing the peaceful conditions of a modern
"Genroku," supported by the growth of the economy. (Genroku,
1688–1704, was a period of peace and prosperity that gave rise
to the merchant class.) Practically, however, Japan differs from
other countries only in that it has reached the stage where income
levels are high enough to allow people to dissipate their day-to-day
frustrations in recreation and pleasure. If in the future rising
demand cannot be adequately fulfilled, it is possible that Japan
will duplicate the pattern that has occurred in other countries.

A sensitive indicator of this trend is the increase in and changing
nature of juvenile crime. In the past the main causes of juvenile
crime were family poverty, some deficiency in the family (such as
only one parent), or a negative environment within or outside the
family. But today families with both parents at home and incomes
well above the poverty level are producing juvenile criminals.
Around 1960, 50 percent or less of the juveniles who came under
the general guardianship of the courts were from families with

both parents; recently this proportion has surpassed 60 percent, while the proportion of juvenile wards from broken families dropped from 35 to below 15 percent. The proportion of juvenile delinquents from families who are poor or needy has decreased from about 65 to 15 percent. Recently the proportion of juvenile criminals from "ordinary" families rose over 80 percent.

These trends in juvenile crime cannot be divorced from the many changes in family life that have occurred since the war, in addition to the permissiveness, overprotection and pampering of children that have accompanied rising incomes and consumption and the spread of small families. Another factor is that, as material life becomes more abundant, young people's wants and expectations also rise, and when their purchasing power cannot satisfy their demands, they are likely to feel thwarted. As a general rule the young are most vulnerable to social imbalances. Their very sensitivity makes them particularly susceptible to the distortions of mass culture. With the increase in the number of students enrolled in institutions of higher education, the ratio of crime by students to all juvenile crime has increased from 50 to 75 percent during the past ten years, while the rate of crime among working juveniles has decreased from 35 to 15 percent of all juvenile crime. This indicates that within the affluent society attained by high economic growth, the mentality of young people has been poorly developed; it also discloses one of the problems in school education.

Juvenile delinquency, destructive or harmful acts which do not amount to crime, is also spreading. Delinquency is a general term applied to problematic conduct and antisocial acts by juveniles. In this limited meaning it applies to crimes committed by youths between 14 and 19, lawbreaking behavior of persons under the age of 14, and juveniles with criminal tendencies who are considered potentially capable of criminal acts in the future. All these are lumped together in the term "delinquents." What is remarkable today is that the juvenile offenders are becoming younger and that they are often committing delinquencies just to amuse themselves. Very often these juveniles have associated with other problem children or groups of delinquents. This trend is evidenced by the fact that, of all the criminal offenses investigated in 1975, almost 40 percent of those by juveniles were committed by two or more persons, which is about three times the rate of multiple-handed offenses by adults. Among them were cases involving gangs of young hoodlums, many of them linked with established gangster groups.

The connection of these gangster groups with crime is an important factor in many aspects of social life. When police control becomes strong, the groups go underground or disperse; when such control is relaxed, they come out into the open again. It is difficult to say whether statistics show the real situation, but if police surveys can be relied on, the number of both gangster groups and gang members have decreased since 1963. However, the number of gang members arrested has been increasing again since 1970, and they are allegedly apt to commit crimes more frequently. The crimes of these gangster groups mainly involve personal injury, intimidation, assault, drug sales and gambling. Of the total number of crimes of intimidation and gambling, 40 percent are gangster crimes. Even more indicative of an ailing society is the growing incidence of blackmail and extortion, whereby a company or organization suffers at the hands of gangsters. Only a few of these cases ever reach the courts. Strong-arm men hired to intimidate stockholders or company representatives are, in this area, only slightly different from gangsters. They are hired to attend general stockholders' meetings disguised as stockholders, to "preserve order" and to "assure" that the meeting proceeds as planned by the directors, with no embarrassing questions or disturbances by the legitimate stockholders.

Drugs and prostitution are a common source of funds for gangs. It was only after the war that drugs became a significant social problem. Drug sales are very strictly controlled and for that reason alone their price is high. The gangs make their way into illicit sales organizations and use this traffic as a source of funds. Gangs formerly were closely connected with prostitution, but since the antiprostitution law went into effect this source of funds has decreased. Prostitution is still difficult to eradicate, and the more strictly it is prohibited, the greater are the potential profits to be gained by clever evasion of the law. Gangs are still involved in such activities.

These darker aspects of society exist in every era; a society without crime or delinquency can hardly be hoped for, but a sound and healthy society can keep them to a minimum. An increasing crime rate is a sign that social development is not keeping pace with economic growth. Although the dark clouds which hang over our society have covered the world since World War II, and even though the situation in Japan is not uniquely bad, our society still has room for improvement.

4. Destruction of the Natural Environment

Japan's economic development has not only aggravated unhealthy social conditions; it has also been destroying the natural environment. This newly dubbed "polluted archipelago" now leads the world in the rate of pollution.

The Japanese word most often used for pollution *(kōgai)* is similar to the English term "public nuisance." Though literally *kōgai* is a calamity inflicted on society as a whole by an unspecified large number of individuals or enterprises, it has come to connote the pollution resulting from the discharge of smoke and water from specified industries. But what is this thing we call *kōgai?*

Pollution long antedates World War II. Exhaust from factories rained soot upon every neighborhood, and smoke from mines stripped the mountains of their verdure. Polluted water contaminated the soil and damaged agricultural products. The soot and smoke of industrial cities were, nonetheless, accepted as symbols of industrial progress, and those who suffered damage had to be content with trifling amounts paid in compensation. From the Meiji period on, the government maintained a policy of increasing production and encouraging industry. The development of mining and manufacturing was considered necessary for the development of Japan, and whatever damage was caused had to be endured. Local governments regarded such damage as a necessary evil to be tolerated for the sake of regional prosperity. The political and social climate allowed industrial enterprises to feel no distress over the pollution they were spreading. The same attitudes

continued after the war. Heavy and chemical industrial growth
and the shift from coal to oil as a source of power increased pollution until discharges from the factories began to destroy the cycle
of nature itself.

Sulfuric acid gas has replaced smoke and dust as the main con-
taminant in polluted air. Industrialized urban areas are so polluted now that, with added exhaust from heating installations and
automobile gases, city people are coughing and gasping for breath
and complaining of smarting eyes from photochemical smog.

Water pollution has also become an urgent problem. Since before the war the lack of adequate sewage systems has contributed to
the contamination of water by household waste. Failure to plan
facilities for disposal of industrial waste, moreover, has turned rivers into sewers and "killed" large areas of our coastal seas. Pollution of rivers is reaching a level where they can no longer purify
themselves naturally. Using rivers as sources of water supply has
required great sums of money for water purification systems, and
in some cases contamination has exceeded the limits beyond which
water cannot be used at all. The waste waters from industrial
plants have passed the stage where they merely damage farm crops
or curtail fishing; they are now eating away at the bodies of human
beings themselves. Such maladies as the Minamata disease and
itai-itaibyō (the "ouch-ouch disease," a bone disease caused by cad-
mium poisoning) are making polluted Japan infamous throughout the world. Extraction of water for industrial use, moreover,
has caused areas of land to sink in some places. The most notable
cases are to be found in Tokyo and Osaka. Noise and vibration
produced by factories, trains, highway transport and other sources
comprise another area of disturbance that is not only destroying
the natural environment but normal human life as well.

Even farm villages, which, if anything, were once the victims
of pollution, have now become the source of pollution. The postwar emphasis on increased production encouraged wide use of
agricultural chemicals and insecticides, and the accumulative
effects has made chemical pollution a serious problem. In addition, the development of recreational areas to attract vast numbers
of tourists is further promoting the destruction of the environment,
as mountains are cleared for roads and land cut up for cheap recreational facilities. If this rate of destruction continues unabated,

the natural environment cannot be preserved, and man's very existence on the soil of Japan may be endangered.

Postwar Japanese governments have been tolerant of environmental destruction, making development of industry their first priority. At a time when rapid increase in production was also causing a rapid increase in pollution, the Ministry of Health and Welfare prepared a bill to prohibit contamination and destruction of the environment. It was pigeonholed as premature. The Water Quality Preservation Law and the Industrial Plant Waste Water Regulations Law came out in 1958; the Soot and Smoke Regulations Law belatedly went into effect in 1962. In 1964 a Pollution Section was established in the Ministry of Health and Welfare. In 1965, when pollution could no longer be ignored, the Pollution Prevention Corporation was formed. Finally, in 1967, the Basic Law on Pollution was drawn up. The Basic Law stressed the need for development of the economy in harmony with nature and set up standards with regard to air, water, and noise levels, but it was not grounded in a basic concern for the people or the country as a whole. Instead, there were noticeable compromises with the existing situation. After a period of extreme pollution, in 1970 the pressure of public opinion succeeded in eliminating those articles in the law which made concessions to economic development. In the same year, revisions and adjustments in the Basic Law on Pollution and other related laws were made, and in 1975 the Natural Environment Preservation Law was enacted. Thus the preservation of the natural environment was finally considered a prime problem whose settlement was urgently needed, and environmental conditions have begun to improve. The argument still persists, nonetheless, that preservation of the environment must be reconciled with sound development of industry—even today the latter tends to be given precedence.

The people of the nation and the residents of polluted areas who have allowed environmental destruction to run its course must bear some of the responsibility for it. The attitude which equates industrial and social development still persists, and popular acquiescence to the destruction of the environment for the sake of the region as a whole has made Japan the most polluted of countries. Both national and local governments have tended to look at the problem from the point of view of the polluting enterprises rather than from that of the citizen. At the present time, concern over pollution has increased; citizens' opposition to the location of polluting industries in their areas has increased considerably, but movements to prevent pollution by established enterprises and demand compensation for damage already caused are very difficult for local residents to promote. Workers in the polluting enterprises hesitate to cooperate with popular movements, knowing that they will be working against their own companies and their own interests. Old established local organizations such as the neighborhood associations are reluctant to join for fear that they will be used for partisan purposes. The soil of Japan, where old social cohesiveness has broken down and where solidarity of regions as democratic communities is a thing of the future, is not fertile ground for citizens' movements. When a proposal is made to strip natural greenery for a new tourist site, most join the destroyers, hoping to share in the profits from the tourist industry, even in the face of conservation-minded opposition.

To preserve the natural environment of Japan and maintain the health of its people, environmental destruction must be stopped and nature must be restored. This will not be easy. Yet despite the predisposition to give priority to the economy, since the 1970 anti-pollution campaign a change has been taking place in the attitude of the Japanese people toward pollution. Court decisions against pollution-causing industries gave impetus to this change. The number of people who now stress the importance of preserving the environment is rapidly growing. The will to preserve the natural environment must take priority and serve to reinforce efforts to provide a complete and enriching life environment. While people have become more aware of the need for the former, there are still very few in our country who can see the connection between the poor efforts being made by politicians, and their lack of desire even to do so, and the provisions such a life environment. It may be a question of political education. Today there are not too many people who have the intention of reforming the socio-political structure of the country; we must encourage many more to think about how our political and economic systems can be used toward a better natural and social environment.

VIII. Economic and Social Development

1. Distorted Development of the Economy

When the economy began to emerge from the immediate post-war chaos around 1950, a comprehensive plan for development was formulated which aimed at developing domestic resources and increasing food production. This was especially important as there were no more colonies to rely on. The plan was directed at development of electric power resources, restoring the mining and manufacturing industries, building multipurpose dams and ultimately expanding the amount of productive land. These measures were intended to restore Japan's devastated territory.

Concentration on developing electric power resources was, in fact, aimed at restoration of the manufacturing industry. Circumstances of the Korean War soon pushed the Japanese economy from a period of restoration into one of growth. The 1955 economic white paper officially declared the end of the "postwar period." All of the groundwork was complete, and it was time to move forward with the building. The growth of manufacturing was remarkable. Steel and petroleum industries utilized new technical innovations and spread their plants to new industrial sites. Their locations were determined according to the most rational ideas of effective production set out in a policy called dispersion of industry, but concentration was almost totally in the Pacific coastal belt. The 1960 Ikeda cabinet income-doubling plan gave little attention to the relocation of these plants. Already existing industrial zones and the Pacific coastal belt were clearly mentioned, while regions whose participation was a possibility were included in a sort of postscript, but most underdeveloped areas were lumped together and dismissed as "other regions."

With the growth of the economy, different regions and industries began to emerge as distinctly more advantageous for growth, until an imbalanced situation became all too obvious. An attempt to balance regional differences was one of the tasks of the 1962 Comprehensive National Development Plan. As is clear from the 1950 Law for the Comprehensive Development of National Territory, which contained the statement, "in addition, [an economic development plan] will contribute to a rise in social welfare," these economic development plans, including the 1962 plan, did not emphasize the welfare of the inhabitants. One advantage of concentration was to accelerate economic growth, but by 1962 the evils of overcrowding were overriding. To correct regional differences meant locating industrial plants in areas outside the Pacific coastal belt to alleviate crowding. It was then that the concept of "new industrial cities" arose. The state was to make the initial investments for an industrial base which would encourage enterprises to move into the established area, or "new city." In substance, this amounted to application of the industry-first principle that favored big business. The welfare of the people was not a principal goal.

At this point it became hard to ignore the distorting effects of economic growth on the lives of the people. The statement of opinions issued by the Population Problems Council in the summer of 1963, entitled "Regional Development and Population Problems," brought this into sharp focus. In it the term "social development" was used for the first time in an official document. The statement stressed the need for social development, using the United Nations concept of "balanced economic and social development," and it criticized the exclusive concentration on economic development which had prevailed until that time.

The next year, in the 1964 election for the Liberal Democratic party presidency, Prime Minister Ikeda proposed correction of social maladjustments as a follow-up to his income doubling plan. He was challenged by Eisaku Satō, who considered Ikeda's measures too weak. Making "social development" his slogan, Satō argued: "In the policy of 'production first,' humanity has been forgotten.

A revival of concern for human life, which has been lost as we grow more prosperous, is a task of the greatest urgency." When Satō succeeded Ikeda as prime minister in fall 1964, he formally proclaimed social development to be the goal of his administration. But the program was never very substantive and finally faded away. There was never any thorough reconsideration of the policy of "production first," and no political shifts occurred to accommodate new thinking. The 1967 Plan for Economic and Social Development explicitly called for attention to social development along with economic, but in actual practice all the emphasis was placed on economic efficiency so as to place Japan in a competitive international position. The first consideration in official thinking was to make the pie larger; i.e., economic growth had to precede welfare.

Unless the pie is large, the reasoning went, the share for each will be too small. But the demand for a larger pie is insatiable, and it is difficult to exercise restraint in productivity ceilings. No one seemed to care about the fact that difficulties, if unattended, will only get worse, regardless of how promising certain economic trends appeared. The growth of Japan's economy has, in effect, been supported by government investments and loans. In 1970, when the gross national product increased to 3.5 times what it was ten years before, the general expenditures were about four times as great, but this increase was far exceeded by treasury investment loans, which rose five times or more. These funds are provided mainly by Postal Ministry savings programs and annuity and insurance reserve funds. They represented the individual savings of the common people, but in the name of public investment they became the foundation for the growth of the economy, built up around large enterprises. Economic growth has increased use of and expenditures for consumer goods, but the proportion of such expenditures in the national economy has dropped from 56 percent in 1960 to about 50 percent in 1970, while investments in plant and equipment have risen from 31 to 36 percent. Compared with the individual expenditures for consumer goods (over 60 percent) and investments in plant and equipment (about 20 percent) in other advanced countries, Japan's investments were extraordinarily high. This was one of the major reasons for the high rate of economic growth. In short, the slogan of social development was empty. No real improvement has been accomplished.

The fine concept of social development requires drastic action to effect substantial economic reform, but the Satō government did not show this kind of courage during its many years in office. Continuing to concentrate on economic development, like the Ikeda government it pushed economic growth under its program of doubling the national income. The high price that had to be paid for priority on economic growth was increased pollution—as became clear to everybody. In 1970 the mass media were playing up the rising levels of pollution, but this was only one problem; many others required urgent attention.

In 1970 the government finally removed the articles that made concessions to economic development from the Basic Law on Pollution and established the Environmental Agency. It also announced a New Economic and Social Development Plan for the period up to 1975, with the subheading, "Toward an Economically Healthy Society Rich in Human Values." The plan stated that the time had come for distributing the pie because the economy now could bear the high cost of providing a high level of welfare. This policy should have been followed long before, but there was no guarantee that the Japanese people would truly benefit. Satō finally had to agree that there could be no growth without welfare, but his successor placed "remodeling the Japanese archipelago" as the main task of government—a concept which was again based on the idea of "economic development first." The year 1973 was said to be the "first year for welfare"; however, retrenchment of welfare policies was already talked about while the slogan was still fresh, since the oil crisis hit the nation in the same year. Such shallowness of welfare policies has made it difficult to attain a high level of welfare.

2. What Social Development Means

The term "social development" originated in a United Nations concept. The Japanese term comes from the English, which was translated as *"shakai kaihatsu,"* with the connotation of "causing to develop." It came into use after a 1957 report of the Economic and Social Council on world social conditions stressed the need for so-cial—as opposed to economic—development, and a 1961 resolution was passed in the UN General Assembly concerning a balance of the two ("balanced economic and social development"). *Shakai kaihatsu* was introduced into Japan as a counterpart to the well-known *keizai kaihatsu* ("economic development").

The United Nations has always promoted economic develop-ment in developing countries, but traditional, cultural and reli-gious factors and low levels of education have blocked rapid de-velopment. This meant that even though industrialization was promoted and modern factories built, it was often impossible to get qualified people to run them, and efforts made to expand agri-culture by eliminating crop-destroying insects were brought to a standstill in some areas by religious taboos on killing insects. It be-came clear during the sixties that unless human capabilities were developed and social conditions were improved, there could be no progress in economic development.

This thinking has been transplanted into Japan, but unlike many countries the UN was then working with, Japan was not a developing country, and measures contemplated by UN bodies were not appropriate. Japan's problem was not the extension of compulsory education, but raising the level of and increasing investments in education; it was not the establishment of a social security system, but that of perfecting that system. Japan, at that time, was "backward" in terms of the gap between social and economic development—it was certainly not "advanced." Japan ranked near the top in production, but it lagged in national income and consumption, and fell even further behind in housing and living environment when compared with other "advanced" countries. Concentration on economic growth at the expense of measures for social development exacerbated social contradictions that were made even more destructive by precipitous economic growth. Thus an originally distorted development process was compounded by the added distortions of the high growth in the postwar period.

Economic development should ultimately be directed toward

the happiness and welfare of the people, but when production takes control the profit motive in a capitalist system tends to rule ruthlessly. Social development founded on the welfare principle and based on the logic of sharing must be counterpoised with economic development in order to regulate the activity of production. If social development is neglected, the rationality of economic development will in the long run become irrational. Social development may involve short-term compromises of economic rationality, but a balance between the two will ultimately be the most satisfactory. Social planning must embrace, therefore, both social and economic development.

The term "social planning" was already in use in the 1930s. Aware of the transition from a free-enterprise, laissez-faire era to one of planning, Karl Mannheim proposed an alternative to both Nazism and communism: "planning for freedom." The necessity for social planning in a capitalist system became clear as the limits to private production and private consumption emerged. Production under a free-enterprise system has become increasingly dependent on social capital, and the rate of public consumption has been rising. Social costs, as opposed to private costs borne by individual corporations, are also mounting. These trends in spending and consumption increase the importance of social development in any kind of broad social planning.

Even Japanese in the political world did not seem to understand social development, though it was much discussed. The business community, which supports the ruling conservative government, also had no vision beyond short-term economic rationality. The social responsibility of business has recently come under discussion but nothing is done about it. Efforts to evade such responsibility are much more clear-cut. Social development is likely to receive only nominal consideration for some time to come, and economic development will continue to dominate planning. To overcome this situation we need a clear understanding of what social overhead capital is. Economic development cannot occur without investment of social capital, but social capital does not simply mean public investment in the production-related sector of the economy. Social capital includes both production investment and investment in living conditions. When development is concentrated on the economy alone, social capital for production gets most attention. This tendency has caused the lag in Japan's social development and the distortion in its economic development. Social capital for production is largely invested in roads, harbors, etc.—things which appear to be for public purposes but mainly serve private enterprise. As the economy develops, moreover, individual consumption reaches a point where it can no longer meet the needs of the people and social or public consumption becomes necessary. But if commensurate investment of social capital for living conditions is not made, economic growth results in deterioration of the living environment.

The people themselves must become sensitive to beneficial ways of investing social capital. If social capital for production is to be invested for the benefit of private enterprise, a fair share of tax revenue from the enterprises must be assured to provide revenue for social capital, and treasury loans must be invested for the improvement of living conditions.

3. Lag in Social Facilities

The rapid growth of the economy has raised the standard of living of the Japanese people. The proportion of individual expenditures for consumption out of total national expenditures dropped to almost 50 percent around 1970 but has recovered to 60 percent in these years of steady growth. Although there was a drop in the rate of growth at one time, total national expenditures have increased enormously, and, making allowance for the rise in prices, total consumption has risen all through the twenty years since the beginning of the high-growth period. One sign of this is the abundance of durable consumer goods in the average home.

The houses in which these goods are used, however, are poor and inadequate. In World War II, 4.2 million dwellings were destroyed. The housing shortage was so great that in the bombed cities air-raid shelters were used as dwellings. Later progress in the construction of housing could not keep up with the demand or the high price of land. The housing crisis continued without change.

At the present time not quite 16 square yards of housing space are available per capita, a little less than 0.8 person per room. The number of housing units built each year has gradually increased, from 600,000 during 1960 to over 1.9 million in 1973, but after the oil crisis it went down and in 1975 it amounted to 1.35 million. Moreover, because of the extraordinary rise in the price of land it is becoming almost impossible for an individual to build his own house. In 1950 the ratio of home ownership was more than 80 percent; at one time this ratio went down to less than half; at present, it is 60 percent. Government housing projects are all the more necessary, but they now account for no more than 45 percent of the annual increase in the number of dwelling units. The standard dwelling unit in a public housing project has been 2DK—a tiny space that may have spurred the transition to the nuclear family. This amount of space allows separate dining and sleeping quarters, but separate bedrooms for children as they become a little older are impossible. In spite of the rise in the level of consumption, stimulated by economic growth, the Japanese people lack a decent living environment in the area most important to them personally—the homes in which they live.

For a family, life outside the home as well as in it needs facilities that can be provided only by public spending. Narrowly defined, these include water supply, sewerage, garbage disposal, utilities, and parks and playgrounds. In a broader sense they also include such educational facilities as nursery schools, kindergartens, schools and libraries; the health and medical facilities of hospitals and health centers; transportation facilities such as highways, streets and buses; and social welfare institutions such as old people's homes. The deficiencies in environmental facilities are many, but to take some examples we can start with water supply. Twenty-five years ago only 25 percent of the population had water piped to their homes. Now the proportion is nearly 90 percent. However, compared with the percentage in other advanced countries, where it is over 90 percent (99 percent in Great Britain), Japan is still backward.

Sewage disposal, compared with that of the advanced countries, is distinctly undeveloped. A little more than 35 percent of the population uses a public sewerage system, compared to 60 percent or more in other advanced countries and 90 percent in Great Britain. Nearly 100 percent of the population now lives in districts that provide disposal systems for human waste, while in 1965 that figure was only 60 percent. This is one reflection of nationwide urbanization. However, the percentage of the population with flush toilets using either sewage systems or septic tanks is 45 percent. An incredible 55 percent still depend on the night-soil men to remove the waste. Conditions of sanitation are better, but disposal facilities in urban areas have not kept up with the population increase: even now 13 percent of all human waste removed from homes is dumped in the ocean. Burnable trash is supposed to be incinerated while nonburnable trash is first crushed or compressed and then disposed of in landfills, but in Japanese cities less than half of all trash is burned, and most goes unprocessed to landfills. The volume of discarded bulky objects, metals and plastics has risen so high recently that we are witnessing a virtual "trash war" in the effort to dispose of it.

Public parks and playgrounds are so scarce that there is no comparison with other advanced countries. Further, public libraries (to say nothing of school libraries) are poorly stocked, and there has been only a small increase in their number. Nursery schools, day-care centers and kindergartens are sorely inadequate. As large number of women seek employment, they face many difficulties holding jobs and simultaneously taking care of their family responsibilities. One problem is the lack of nursery schools. There are more than there used to be, but this is still not enough, and their facilities are generally meager. The facilities and personnel of unlicensed ones — those not passing certain set standards — are inadequate, even though they compensate somewhat for the lack in numbers. In medical care and health facilities Japan ranks with other leading countries in number of hospital beds. The number of doctors is also almost as high as in other countries, but there is a noticeable shortage of nurses. The main problem is that medical facilities tend to cluster in the cities, leaving rural, mountain and fishing villages with little medical care. This maldistribution of medical facilities and doctors adds to the insecurity of people living in remote areas, but no new measures to help medically-deprived regions are being taken. While there seems to have been progress in the construction of express highways and trunk roads, the proportion of paved roads is far lower than in other advanced countries, and we have come to understand that road improvements designed only for greater automobile traffic are actually a factor damaging to human life. Again, the need for balance between efficiency and welfare must be thoroughly reconsidered.

The lag in these environmental facilities is one result of a prewar disregard for the investment of social capital in living conditions. That neglect was carried over into the postwar period, and even now Japan's living conditions measure up to about two-thirds those of other advanced countries. Japan now faces the task of overcoming the inadequacy of social investment. Recent investments in living environment facilities have increased, compared to those during the period of high economic growth; they must be increased several times over to achieve a balance between income and welfare.

Adequate social development demands at least a curtailment of rapid economic growth, and investment in social overhead capital for production must be transformed into that for living. Increases in military defense expenditures must be abandoned. If the country can concentrate on providing adequate facilities for the living environment, part of the Japanese stigma of being called "economic animals," intent only on economic growth, will be lifted. The fear that Japan is reviving militarism may also fade. But is there any possibility of this?

4. Low Level of Social Security

The Constitution of Japan provides that: "All citizens have the right to live in good health, and at a certain minimum level of culture." It goes on to say that the nation "must strive for an increase in social security and public health." Thus, whereas before the war social security was limited to relief and charity, after the war it became institutionalized as the right of every citizen.

The term "social security" in its broad sense has a variety of meanings. The Advisory Council on Social Security, in its recommendations issued in 1950 stated:

Social security means a certain guarantee that the suffering of illness, injury, childbirth, disability, death, old age, too many children, and other causes of poverty will be alleviated through an insurance program or direct public assistance. It also means providing state aid for those who have fallen into straitened circumstances, thereby guaranteeing them a minimum standard of living. Its aim is to raise the level of public health and social welfare, thus enabling every citizen to live as a worthy member of a cultured society.

This is a fairly broad definition of social security, but according to its narrower, generally accepted meaning, social security, with public aid and social insurance as its main components, is a public system to guarantee a certain level of income and medical care.

Public aid in the guarantee of livelihood *(seikatsu hogo)* discussed earlier is not a system of charitable relief. It aims at guaranteeing the citizen's right to a living and promoting his ability to be independent and self-supporting. Benefits under it are varied, including certain living expenses, help in education, housing, medical care, childbirth, occupation, and funerals. Though the level of social security has been rising year after year, there remains a great difference between the living expenditures of ordinary families and those receiving this assistance. The latter receive only half as much as the former are able to spend. Because funds for assistance come from general revenue sources in the national and local governments, they are covered by taxes paid by the citizens. Hence, balance between livelihood assistance and social insurance is necessary. The low level of social insurance programs reflects a low level of security guarantee. In the famous Asahi case, which was argued for a period of ten years beginning in 1956, a complaint by Shigeru Asahi was filed contesting the demand that he bear part of the cost of the medical care he received. The issue became the contention that the standard of protection of the Livelihood Security Law was in violation of Article 25 of the Constitution. In the end the lawsuit was dismissed.

Social insurance in Japan has had a very brief history. It is a system supposed to provide a guaranteed income against loss of earnings due to old age, disability, on-the-job accidents, occupational diseases and unemployment, and also to pay medical care expenses for injuries or illness. However, in our country there is a complicated network of welfare annuity insurance, national annuities, health insurance, day laborers' insurance, national health insurance, unemployment insurance, workmen's accident compensation insurance, seamen's insurance and all kinds of mutual benefit associations (of national and local public service workers, employees of public corporations, private school teachers, and employees of farming, forestry and fishing organizations). All were established at various times and differ from one another in character and the level of service they provide.

The annuity systems may be divided into two major categories: the occupational group systems (such as welfare annuity insurance and seamen's insurance, and mutual benefit association annuities), and the regional annuities of the national annuity system. By the 1959 National Annuity Law the latter brought those left out of other annuity systems into the regional insurance system. With this, Japan finally has an annuity structure that has included everyone since 1961. Japan's annuity systems as a whole have been established for only a short time, however, and benefits were paid only beginning in 1971. Even the Employees' Welfare Annuity Insurance has been in existence for only about thirty-five years. It was preceded by the Workmen's Annuity Insurance of 1942, but that was established as a device for raising funds for military expenditures rather than for workers' welfare. The level of annuity was very low, but in the 1972 general election the annuity system became a point of dispute. With the revision of laws in fiscal 1973, the level of annuity was raised and an indexing annuity system was introduced. As a result, the welfare annuity is now about 130,000 yen a month. The national annuity, which was 2,000 yen a month at the beginning, has also risen to 84,000 yen for a husband and wife combined, after the couple has paid welfare annuity premiums for the standard period. Comparing this amount with the annuities paid in other advanced countries, it is not at all low. However it will be more than ten years before the first group of people will benefit from this amount of national annuity. Moreover, considering the high prices of commodities, our annuities are not adequate yet, even if the nominal amount is comparable to that of other countries. The level of the annuities must be raised further. There should also be adjustment of the inequities among the systems, of which there are now too many. In the future the number of aged will increase rapidly, and the obligations upon younger generations to support the aged cannot but become severer. Where to set the basic level of the annuity is a difficult problem, but it should be high enough to enable people in their old age to maintain somehow a minimum standard of living by means of their annuities.

From a survey of popular savings, as shown in Table 25, one can understand the situation of the Japanese who strives as hard as he can to save money, and one sympathizes with his fear of the life he faces in his old age. A speedy improvement of the annuities is what most people are calling for. In one survey of workers' attitudes toward living conditions, over 60 percent said they wanted much further development of social security.

Table 25. Savings and Debts (1979) (in units of ¥10,000)

		No. in household	Number employed	Age of head	Annual income	Savings	Debts	Debts for house & land
All households surveyed:		3.83	1.51	44.8	431.4	521.2	170.8	138.3
Grouped by income level:	I	3.30	1.14	46.5	189.9	256.4	53.6	35.9
	II	3.72	1.39	41.1	294.3	329.0	88.8	73.7
	III	3.93	1.50	42.5	374.3	409.1	158.8	135.0
	IV	4.05	1.61	44.9	478.1	537.2	216.6	184.2
	V	4.16	1.92	48.7	820.2	1,037.5	335.8	263.0

Public health and medicine are likewise complicated. Not only are there differences between the medical care insurance provided by occupational groups and that provided by national health insurance, but generally in private business enterprises which employ 100 or more persons there is a recognized company health insurance program. In relatively large enterprises, the workers are enrolled in programs managed by an independent health insurance association, while those in small enterprises take government-administered health insurance. As a reflection of the difference in wage levels, the former are able to collect more in insurance premiums than the latter, can pay benefits in addition to those fixed by law, and are able to build and operate health and recreation facilities. National health insurance, because the premiums collected are low and the share of the cost borne by the national and local governments is great, provides only limited benefits. Such discrepancies in quality between the various insurance systems are in need of drastic reform.

In sum, Japan's social security—public assistance and social insurance—is not very different from that of other advanced countries, if we judge from increased expenditures on it. The addition of a program of allowances for children in 1972 has made the whole social security system complete. However, while the rate of increase of expenditure has been relatively high, steps to improve a very poor social security system are entirely unsatisfactory. There are still many who are living in insecurity in a "valley" of the social security system due to its incompleteness. The ratio of the total expenditures for social security to gross national product has improved from 4.5 percent in 1960 to about 10 percent. This ratio can scarcely be compared with the 20–30 percent of Western European countries. Japan's annuities still have a long way to go to even approximate the level in other advanced countries. As our per capita income is now ranked with that of Great Britain, we can no longer excuse our backwardness on the grounds of inadequate experience with social security.

IX. Conservative and Reform Forces

1. Postwar Japanese Politics

Postwar politics were grounded in policies established between 1945 and the year the occupation ended, 1952, when the Japanese-American security structure was set up and the peace treaty was signed. During that time the American Occupation carried out a great many reforms in all areas with an aim to democratization and the eradication of militarism. Big industrial conglomerates—*zaibatsu*—were dissolved and a thorough land reform was carried out; the right of labor to organize was recognized and the secret police was abolished. Women were given political rights, and the six-three-three system of education was introduced. The new Constitution of Japan became the legal protection of the reforms. Among other changes, the prewar conservative parties, Seiyūkai and Minseitō, reappeared in revised form. Reformist parties, which had little power before the war, made remarkable gains under the policy of democratization. Shortly after the war a coalition government of socialist and conservative parties gained control.

Deepening Cold War tensions and the outbreak of the Korean War caused the Occupation to shift its focus sharply from the "experiment in democracy" to creating in Japan a "bulwark against communism." With the fall of the reformist-conservative coalition government and the complete victory of the Liberal party (Jiyūtō) in the 1949 election, Japanese political leaders turned their efforts toward revising the democratic institutions which had been built up on the basis of the new Constitution. This trend became known as "reverse course." It created a situation wherein the conservative parties wanted "reform" of Occupation policy and reformist parties, wanting to "preserve" the Constitution, were "conservative."

In the first postwar decade, there was a complex multiparty situation in which alliances among both conservative and reformist parties shifted many times. The Imperial Rule Assistance Association, into which all prewar political parties had been merged during the war, fell apart completely. A massive purge of wartime office-holders followed, and their gradual rehabilitation heightened the complexity and fluidity of the political scene. The multiparty period came to an end in 1955 when the faction-ridden Socialist party regained unity and the conservative parties combined into the Liberal Democratic party (LDP). The latter merger was pushed by Japanese financial and industrial leaders. Due to the special procurement demand created by the Korean War, industry was restored and beginning to grow. The economic white paper of 1956, referring to the preceding year, declared: "The postwar period is over." It was in this white paper that the term "innovation" of technology first appeared in conjunction with the vision of economic growth.

The beginning of economic growth also marked the beginning of an era of political confrontation between two major parties, the conservative and the reformist. Because of the wide gap in strength, it was more like a one-and-a-half-party system than typical two-party politics. This unbalanced two-party system lasted only a few years, however. Unable to break the overwhelmingly strong control of the conservative party, reform elements were barely able to maintain a little over one-third of the seats in the Diet, a force necessary to prevent the conservative majority from revising the Constitution, especially Article 9 renouncing war and rearmament. In the meantime, factional rivalry within the Socialist party intensified until a right-wing faction broke off and formed a new party, the Democratic Socialist party, in January 1960. Another new party, the Clean Government party (Kōmeitō), appeared in 1964; also the Communist party began to grow, giving rise to a multiparty political alignment. A divided opposition naturally solidified the conservatives' domination all the more thoroughly.

The basic policy of the Liberal Democratic party government has been to preserve the Japanese-American security system and, if the opportunity should arise, to revise the Constitution. Its reactionary character was most strongly revealed during 1960 when the Kishi cabinet railroaded through ratification of the revised security treaty. This provoked a huge popular protest against such high-handed tactics, and Kishi was forced to resign. Thereafter, extolling the benefits of the Japanese-American security system, the conservative government went in wholehearted pursuit of economic growth. As a result, the gross national product rose steadily, along with national income and the level of consumption. Remarkable changes were occurring in the social structure: Japan was developing into a mass society. This resulted in a larger new middle class, a narrowing of the discrepancies between white- and blue-collar workers, greater political apathy, and a growing trend toward withdrawal from politics. The backdrop for these changes in the social structure was the period of political tranquility under conservative governments during the 1960s. Both rural communities and the old middle class section of the cities remained strong bases of support for the conservative party. In contrast, a lack of interest in and withdrawal from politics was spreading among the working class. While extraordinary economic growth brought about a rise in the level of consumption, it could not improve the quality of life in general. In a sense, this imbalance gave rise to a new feeling of poverty. A higher level of consumption produced frustrated desires, and people began to realize that as long as they just sought escape in their private lives, there would be no real improvement in overall living conditions. As people grew aware of the lag in social facilities and the insidious effects of pollution, they became increasingly disenchanted with the conservative regime. This is manifested in the fact that from 1967 on the conservative party has failed to gain even half the popular vote, although it has retained a Diet majority partly because of imbalances in the rural-urban apportionment of seats.

The reformists were unable to respond effectively to this shift. The Socialist party, their main force, did not take advantage of a widespread feeling of alienation and the issue of the deteriorating environment by attacking the conservative government, calling for broader reform, and intensifying popular disenchantment with conservatism. The hope for a Socialist government was bright

Table 26. Shifts in Election Results: House of Representatives

		May 1958	Nov. 1960	Nov. 1963	Jan. 1967	Dec. 1969	Dec. 1972	Dec. 1976	Oct. 1979	June 1980
Liberal Democratic party	No. of seats won	287	296	283	277	288	271	249	253	286
	Percentage of votes	57.8	57.5	54.6	48.8	47.6	46.9	41.8	44.6	47.9
Socialist party	No. of seats won	166	145	144	140	90	118	123	107	107
	Percentage of votes	32.9	27.5	29.0	27.8	21.4	21.9	20.7	19.7	19.3
Democratic Socialist party	No. of seats won	—	17	23	30	31	19	29	36	33
	Percentage of votes	—	8.7	7.3	7.4	7.7	7.0	6.3	6.8	6.6
Kōmeitō	No. of seats won	—	—	—	25	47	29	55	58	34
	Percentage of votes	—	—	—	5.3	10.9	8.4	10.9	9.8	9.0
Communist party	No. of seats won	1	3	5	5	14	38	17	41	29
	Percentage of votes	2.6	2.9	4.0	4.7	6.8	10.5	10.4	10.4	9.8
New Liberal Club	No. of seats won	—	—	—	—	—	—	17	4	12
	Percentage of votes	—	—	—	—	—	—	4.1	3.0	3.0

during the reconstruction period but the party never grew strong enough to break through its minority position. In the latter half of the 1960s the limitations of a labor-union-sponsored party became clear, and the party began to decline. Gains by other opposition parties made up for the decline, but the shift toward a multiparty situation only decreased the percentage of votes received by the Liberal Democratic party; it did not succeed in reducing the conservative strength in the Diet. However, in the general elections held at the end of 1975, partly because of the secession of the New Liberal Club (NLC) from the Liberal Democratic party, the LDP's strength in the House of Representatives declined and the conservatives and the opposition became nearly equal in the House of Representatives. Now the situation is the same in the House of Councillors; but even so, the door to forming a government is still not open for the reformists.

2. Mechanisms of Conservative Control

Japan's conservative party is closely linked with big business interests. Before the war the Seiyūkai was also linked with the Mitsui *zaibatsu*, and the Minseitō with Mitsubishi. But in prewar politics the power of the Genrō (elder statesmen) and the Privy Council under the imperial political system was great enough to counterbalance the government to some extent. There was also a powerful, though slowly declining, landlord class which constituted a major factor in prewar politics. But after the war the authority of the prime minister became very great. To become allied with this authority, to be able to manipulate it, brought direct benefits. Thus the big financial interests became actively and closely involved in politics.

Postwar liquidation of the *zaibatsu* and purges of leaders in the financial world limited the power of big financial interests. They then tried to align themselves with the government in order to get government funds. With the signing of the peace treaty, the end of the Occupation and the rebuilding of Japan's economy, such organizations as the Federation of Economic Organizations (*Keidanren*), the Japan Federation of Employers' Associations (*Nikkeiren*), the Japan Chamber of Commerce and Industry (*Nisshō*) and the Japan Committee for Economic Development (*Keizai Dōyūkai*) became strong pressure groups, or "managers" in politics. The power of these four organizations operated to bring about the merger of the two conservative parties in 1955 and later to effect a reconciliation between factions in the party. The Liberal Democratic party embraces members whose political views are so different that they might be divided into two parties; they have remained together until recently not only because they are intent on maintaining their political power but also because the big financial interests have strongly inhibited any split. These groups make large political contributions to the party in the form of corporate donations, and at the same time receive large sums in treasury investment loans and favorable tax treatment from the government. People are beginning to wonder what mechanism enables the LDP to have maintained its majority in the Diet.

First let us look at the rural communities, the "impregnable castle" of the LDP. After surviving postwar agrarian land reforms, these communities became something quite different from the prewar farm villages. The system by which farmers automatically vote for candidates supported by landlords is no longer operative. Whom they vote for now depends on the persuasive powers of village leaders, and their votes go to candidates who best seem to represent local interests. Issues do not affect their voting; it is the candidate who helps get local roads and bridges built and repaired and on whom they can rely for bond issues and subsidies that gets their votes. These candidates make campaign pledges to work for the local area. To make sure of the farm vote, they are constantly promoting ties with it. They organize associations of supporters, keep in touch with local leaders who are members, and promise them all kinds of favors. They get members of the prefectural assembly into their chain of personal contacts, and through them get city, town and village assembly members into their organization. They also provide financial assistance for the election of these members of local assemblies.

Such activity requires large sums of money that cannot be covered by a dietman out of his salary. The political base is cultivated with funds collected by the party itself from the political fund-raising groups of large financial interests and by leaders of the faction to which the candidate belongs. The mayors of cities, towns and village and influential members of assemblies which are in the candidate's constituency can expect rewards if their districts give him a large vote, and in return he will make special efforts for their localities in petitions to the government. Through this mechanism local leaders are made to feel as if they are important political figures. Their positions as "influential" people are confirmed if they will play an active part in the vote-getting network of the dietman.

Almost the same mechanism operates in the old middle class sections of the cities. The dearth of public facilities in Japan's cities provides the numerous city and ward assemblymen, mainly independent proprietors, with many tasks to do for the local neighborhood associations, in the "gutter-cover assemblyman" tradition. They are links in the prefectural assemblyman's chain of personal connections, and through this they are members of dietmen's support organizations. Through personal connections they can hold their positions as city or ward assemblymen and enjoy the satisfaction of sharing in national politics. To attain that, however, they have to make strenuous efforts for the election of the candidate who is at the top of the connection chain. Traditional urban society, along with the rural communities, forms part of the base of conservatism.

As noted in Chapter IV, however, the larger a city becomes the less secure is the urban conservative base. On the one hand, the living environment of the cities has been deteriorating, and on the other, traditional urban communities are beginning to break up and the relative importance of employed workers has been increasing. The vote-getting power of local conservative assemblymen has been declining. The independent small-shop and local-factory owners who are not benefiting from rapid economic growth are deserting leaders of neighborhood associations. An increasing number are joining organizations of Kōmeitō and the Communist party. The Liberal Democratic party's share of the votes in the country as a whole has dropped to less than half, while in the large cities it has fallen to 30 percent or less, a striking indication of the shrinking conservative base.

Nevertheless, the conservative support base still remains in regional cities. Changes in the very large cities do not have much overall effect because under the election-district system the proportion of such districts in the rural prefectures is large. Until changes in the large cities extend to local cities, there will probably be no sudden change in the majority of the conservative party, including all the offshoots, in the Diet, even though the percentage of votes received by the Liberal Democratic party has been as low as 40 percent. Thus, it might be possible for the opposition parties to obtain a majority in the Diet, but they cannot be expected to surpass the conservatives. Most cities, except for the very large ones, do not tend to vote for reformist mayors. Conservatism is dominant; the further from big urban centers the stronger its hold, and thus its support of political control by the LDP.

Thus, the course of the Japanese conservative party continues to be promotion of policies that suit the purposes of its managers (the big financial interests) and cultivation of its electoral base by taking care of certain minor interests of local areas. This political course has consistently focused on economic growth, on whole-hearted efforts to make the pie larger. As the pie became larger through rapid economic growth, the social structure of Japan changed. The old middle class, which remained the base of support for the conservative party, decreased in size, while the new middle class grew; the members of this new middle class are neither reformists nor constituents of the vote-getting mechanism of the conservative party. The theory that if anyone wants "a slice of the pie" he must cooperate to make the pie larger is no longer acceptable to the new middle class. As a result of such changes in the structure of the bases of support for the conservative party, it has become more fashionable to talk about "priority for welfare" and to play down economic growth, but the party will not easily change the direction it has so long taken. "Regard for human life" and "priority for living conditions" are currently popular terms, but, far from becoming a reality, they seem to be empty phrases. The era of big-business egoism is over, but the party's basic course seems to remain unchanged, on both the national and local levels.

Although they speak publicly of obligation to increase incomes in the prefecture and in their cities, towns and villages, local governments have conformed to the national policy of economic growth—to achieve high returns from investment, and to attract factories to their areas with the primary aim of expanding sources of revenue. Efforts to achieve these goals have been supported by conservative members of local assemblies. They are loyal to certain members of the Diet. This kind of local assemblyman finds himself in a position where he must oppose relocation of pollution-causing industrial plants in his area, for example, but his basically conservative orientation is too strong for him to change rapidly.

3. Reformists' Conservative Response

Japan's reformist parties were only weak, small factions before the war. They blossomed after 1945, encouraged by the wave of democratization and political support from the newly formed labor unions. The Socialist party split for a time but was reunited in 1955, and in the election held shortly before reunification took place, the leftist faction made great progress. The united Socialist party alone won one-third of the seats in the House of Representatives, surpassing the Democratic party, the smaller of the two conservative parties. This stimulated merger of the conservative parties, creating what looked like an era of true two-party politics.

The Socialist party (JSP) was expected to make further gains, but these hopes were disappointed. Liberal Democrats capitalized on Socialist weaknesses and, to build up their own power, refrained from pushing the inflammatory issue of constitutional revision, concentrating instead on economic growth. Thus the basic tenet of the socialist platform—preserving the Constitution—lost its force when the LDP failed to push revision of the Constitution. The party's insistence on the outdated dogma that a socialist revolution inevitably results from the depression of the working class appeared anachronistic in view of the rapid economic growth that technological innovations had made possible. The Socialist party was unable to produce a political program to correspond with the changes in society brought by industrialization, nor did it make any efforts to broaden the base of its support.

Leaders of reformist parties just after the war were part of the prewar socialist movement, but gradually their role was taken over by trade-union activists who had turned to politics. Union support of the party increased and the party became established as virtually a labor union party. Though unions formed the party's support base, they were never brought together into a unified group, and since the secession of the Democratic Socialist party, the JSP has controlled only half of the nation's unionized workers, who are about 31 percent of the total. In medium-sized election districts (constituencies which elect more than one Diet member) the Socialist party generally had only one candidate; they did not have to face the problem of the LDP, wherein several candidates vied with one another, ultimately fostering the formation of intraparty factions. However, conflicts among national labor groups in support of different candidates were reflected in the Socialist party itself, and it was difficult to unite the party toward common goals. Energy was wasted in struggles for leadership between left-wing and right-wing·factions. Moreover, rising wages served to dampen worker interest in reform or party politics. As we have seen in Chapter V, the workers were oriented chiefly toward their company, and the system of company unions created no conflict for them between loyalty to company and union. This "corporate egoism" was a barrier to the solidarity of organized labor, and there was little interest in forming a broad front with unorganized workers to break down the mechanism of conservative domination. Tne labor movement initiated by the Government and Public Workers Union even widened the gap between organized and unorganized workers.

Support for the Socialist party, therefore, far from increasing, remained stagnant and later even began to decline. The party responded only weakly to the needs of farmers, many of whom were turning into blue-collar workers with the advance of industrial development. The party urged that the benefits of growth be brought to the farmers also, but in actual practice went no further than to support raising of the price of rice. Such a weak policy was ineffective in gaining support for the JSP among farmers. It represented an opportunity missed, for the conservatives' policy of restructuring agriculture meant discarding poor farmers. The socialists should have foreseen changes in the structure of rural society, and should have assured farmers that unlike the government party it would find ways to create employment opportunities for them so that even if they left the farms they could get jobs without having to worry. They should also have appealed to the workers, who were enjoying higher levels of pay and consumption, warning them that if they were satisfied with their own improved circumstances and failed to cooperate with unorganized labor, there could be no real rise in the overall standard of living. The party could also have made more effort to check the tendency for union leaders to use the national Diet as a place of comfortable retirement.

Socialist politicians did not use their opportunity for serious efforts to enlist unorganized labor and independent proprietors. Support from the new urban middle class might have been stronger if the party had anticipated the problems to society of increased concentration on "production first." Instead, it did nothing about the deteriorating environment and the drastic increase in pollution, and made no effort to organize citizens' movements to combat them. The party should not have opposed annuities for all citizens under the national annuity system but should have promised a higher level of social security than the conservative party, with a concrete program to achieve this.

No policies or actions that responded to the development of a new social and economic structure were forthcoming from the Socialist party—the labor union party. Its top-heavy organization made it just another parliamentarian party, incapable of moving beyond a formalistic program. In a sense, there was no way for reformist "conservatism" to oppose conservative "reform."

The base of support for the Socialist party grew even weaker when the Democratic Socialist party split off, and the Kōmeitō made a successful appeal to old-middle-class independent proprietors threatened by the prospect of declining into the proletariat. Thus, while conservative support remained steady, support for the Socialist party began to erode. The tendency now is toward multiple opposition parties.

In the general elections at the end of 1972 the Socialist party began to emerge from its decline and to some extent recovered its strength in the Diet, but in the 1975 elections there was no further increase. Rather, the percentage of votes received by the party declined from that of 1972, and according to public opinion surveys support for the party has continued to decrease. This tendency was even more accelerated in the House of Councillors elections in 1977 when a new faction, the United Social Democratic party, split off from the JSP. It is not at all certain that the JSP can regain full strength.

The postwar advance of another reformist party, the Communist party, was cut off by the switch in Occupation policy toward making Japan a bastion against communism. The party further spoiled a chance to expand its influence by the mistaken tactics of extreme left-wing adventurism. After a long period of stagnation when there was no increase in Communist representation in the Diet, its organization again began to expand, and it grew as the Socialist party declined. In the 1972 general elections 38 members were elected to the House of Representatives and the party moved into second place among the opposition parties. However, in the 1975 general elections the party lost a considerable number of its Diet seats, even though the percentage of votes received by the party remained the same. The JCP not only allowed the Kōmeitō to run ahead again but also fell behind the Democratic Socialist party. In the two elections to the House of Representatives which followed, the party obtained fluctuating results.

In contrast to the feeble Socialist grass-roots organization, the Communist party organization works effectively on a regular day-to-day basis. A general prejudice against the Communist party was carried over from the prewar days under the emperor system and was strengthened by tactical mistakes after the war, but efforts to dispel that prejudice seem to be bearing fruit. However, it still contains in itself an intrinsic barrier to expansion—the instinct to protect the organizational sovereignty of the party, or party egoism.

There were many who were dissatisfied with the Communist party as it was and also disappointed in the Socialist party. These formed the core of extremist groups outside the system, the so-called New Left. There was a considerable segment of the population which, though it did not approve of the extremism, sympathized with this movement as an expression of rebellion against the present political and economic system. While some people were smug and unconcerned with politics, there were many in the younger generation, among supporters of the Socialist party in particular, who deserted the declining party to support the New Left—too many to be ignored. However, since the early seventies, these anti-Establishment extremists have dissipated their energy in interfaction conflicts and lost popular support.

The reformist parties do not seem able to muster either the force or the programs to absorb the energy of this element deserting the old left. Both the Socialist and the Communist parties lack the magnetism to concentrate on the new middle class who have always been supporters of the conservative party but now are not interested in any particular party. There is a certain limit to the future spread of the more moderate Democratic Socialist party, which is dependant on the *Dōmei*, nor is the Kōmeitō likely to expand further since it seems to have already obtained almost all the support it can win; development of the so-called middle-of-the-road reformists can scarcely be expected. The road ahead of the reformist parties in Japan is still very rough.

4. Prospects for Reform

The LDP has been in control of politics and government for all of the postwar period, except for the brief period of confusion immediately after the war. Will this power continue? When the economy began to grow, even some of the Liberal Democratic "new right" thought that the growing numbers of workers would eventually mean government by a reformist party. Socialist party leaders were also convinced they would gain control. Actual events turned out otherwise, however. The "one-and-a-half party system" continued unchanged, and the power of the reformist parties grew even weaker as the opposition parties proliferated. Until recently the conservative-dominated political structure showed no signs of changing. Suspending its goal of the late fifties to amend the Constitution, the conservative party in 1960 adopted a "low profile" and concentrated on doubling national income. By more than doubling economic growth it has established itself as a stable political power. This extraordinary growth created such social distortions, however, that even the prime minister, who had advocated income doubling, was forced to acknowledge the need for corrective measures. The succeeding cabinet, moreover, came in on a platform calling for change in the old policy and more attention to social development, but it soon reverted to the policy of its predecessors. The result was even higher economic growth, Japan's GNP ranking third in the world. As the level of consumption rose, the illusion prevailed until the end of the 1960s that Japan was successfully becoming an "advanced" country. The foundations of conservative power seemed firm, even though there was a slight decrease in its support. Most people enjoyed the feeling of prosperity and the high rate of mass consumption, but social problems grew more serious. Today we are keenly aware of the steady accumulation of polluted water and air, and the lack of public facilities for living is at least becoming intolerable to an increasingly urbanized and sophisticated populace. It is now seen that the higher income responsible for greater consumption is offset by steady rises in consumer goods prices. The increase in land prices, generally greater than other prices, has created a bottleneck in housing development and heightened dissatisfaction. People may enjoy what they can buy now, but many are apprehensive about their old age. In 1970 there was a strong desire on the part of the people to start the new decade with a new constructive policy, but there was no call for a shift from the conservative government itself. LDP support reached its lowest point toward the end of the Satō cabinet, which had been in power for an unusually long time.

The conservative party has been saved by the electoral system from losing power as it loses support. It has been able to maintain an absolute majority in the Diet even though its share of the total vote has dropped below 50 percent. Nonetheless, there has been a marked change in general voting behavior since the begining of the 1970s, and this is especially noticeable in the large cities. In the Tokyo gubernatorial election a landslide victory for the reformist candidate jolted the conservative dream of perpetual political power. Conservative defeats in large cities in the 1971 local elections added to that shock. City dwellers had not necessarily become reformist, but their dissatisfaction with living conditions moved them to support candidates who took the side of the people. Thus they elected reformist municipal governments.

The conservative agricultural administration had steadily raised the price of rice, at the same time avoiding any genuinely constructive measures. It was then forced to cope with a rice surplus. Cultivated acreage was limited as a means of regulating rice production, as the result support in the farm villages began to decline. This was reflected in the 1971 elections to the House of Councillors. In the December 1972 House of Representatives elections, the Liberal Democratic party recouped some of its losses owing to the previously mentioned vote-getting mechanism, but in the 1975 elections it won only about half of the seats in the Diet. The gaining of a majority by the opposition parties in the House of Councillors did not take place in the 1977 elections, but it was expected in later elections. However, this does not necessarily mean that support for the conservatives has declined and that for the reformists has increased, as is proved by the support gained by a new faction of the conservatives, the New Liberal Club, which has split away from the LDP in protest against its money politics.

The Liberal Democratic party won an overwhelming victory in the 1980 general elections and is still the largest in the Diet, far exceeding the others in the number of seats; a change of regime now seems unlikely to occur unless the LDP dissolves itself.

Nevertheless, conservative politics must take a new direction. In recent elections the LDP has called for measures to improve standards of welfare and a shift toward emphasizing the environment and a better society. But slogans alone are not enough. The party must carry out the policies it talks about if the decline in its support is to be curbed. Even the big business interests that support the conservatives can no longer ignore demands for humane practices and will probably be forced to consider concessions. From now on measures for social development will probably be promoted more than ever before.

This does not mean that political reform will develop out of any conservative concessions to reality. The outlook for reformism in politics is not a bright one, because even though the conservative party may make some policy shifts, its essential character and pro-business orientation will not allow any complete change of priorities to social development.

In order to force the conservative party to set about "social development" in real earnest, the reformist parties must become stronger. These parties are now trying to establish a reformist regime through a united front, but while the Communist party envisages a Communist-Socialist leadership in such a front, the other opposition parties favor a formula by which all minority parties pledge to cooperate on agreed issues. Unless greater efforts by the reformist parties can strengthen the trend toward liberalizing the conservative party and serve as a brake to rightist inclinations, there is no hope for Japanese politics.

It cannot be expected in the next few years that the politics of the 1970s will bring about the formation of a reformist coalition government, but when that possibility arises, the conservative party must be compelled to "reform" its basic policies. Otherwise, there is little prospect for the reformation of Japanese politics.

Conclusion: The Future for Japanese Society

1. End of "GNP-ism"

In the preceding ten chapters I have discussed some of the problems of modern Japanese society. In conclusion, I should like to reflect once more on the course postwar Japan has taken up till now and on the course that, hopefully, Japanese society will follow in the future.

The defeat in 1945 was, in effect, a "second opening" of the country. Following the first opening over a century ago Japan set out to increase the nation's wealth and strengthen its armed forces, to catch up with the advanced Western countries as rapidly as possible.

In 1945 Japan's leaders should have thoroughly reconsidered the path their country took after the first opening, but they failed to see the crucial significance of August 15, 1945. Having renounced all military power, Japan concentrated exclusively on a rush to add to its wealth. Before one became aware of it the so-called Self-Defense Force had come into being, but compared with the prewar cost of armed forces, military expenditure was slight. Public investment was promoted to develop the production base, and Japan's economy grew. The measuring rod for the enrichment of the country was the GNP.

In 1960, a few years after the beginning of the growth period, the GNP was about equal to that of Italy and behind that of the U.S.A., the U.S.S.R., West Germany, Great Britain and France. This put Japan's GNP in sixth or seventh place. However, its average annual per capita income of $341 ranked it only in about 30th place. In this period the term "GNP" was not yet widely known and most people were striving to acquire the "Three Sacred Treasures." Most roads were uneven and bumpy, and dust-covered bus passengers felt that they were just barely crawling up from the abject defeat in the war.

Very soon the high rate of economic growth caused production to increase; efforts to give priority to industry were producing results. In 1965 the national per capita income doubled to $680, and Japan's GNP rose to a level with Great Britain and France in competition for fourth place. From that time on the GNP became a kind of fetish for Japanese. The tradition dating back to the Meiji period of overtaking and surpassing the leading countries still survived.

Then in 1968 Japan's GNP finally surpassed that of West Germany and moved into second place in the "free world," or third in the whole world, behind only the U.S.A. and the U.S.S.R. In per capita income Japan was still under 15th but to reach third place in GNP was a flattering turn of event for the Japanese people. At the beginning of the same year a manpower survey revealed that less than 20 percent of the population was engaged in agriculture. This was taken as an indication that Japan had reached the level of the "advanced" countries. It was a period when an optimistic "futurology" was offering any number of visions about the years to come. But while "vision" means "foresight" and "insight," it also means "dream" and "illusion." Such visions and talk of the future have the danger of making people oblivious to present reality.

These dreams did not last long. Priority to production sustained the high rate of growth, but with growth, society was sunk even deeper in serious contradictions. The deterioration in living conditions and destruction of the natural environment shattered the GNP idol. Recent economic stagnation degraded the idol all the more.

A major newspaper went so far as to run a series of feature stories entitled "To hell with GNP!" An increase in the GNP is not bad in itself. There can be no increase in national income without an increase in the GNP. While Japan is third in GNP, it is only about 15th in per capita national income; to raise that ranking is not a bad thing. But most Japanese overlook the fact that, although Japan is third in GNP, a population of more than one hundred million brings the per capita income down to only about 15th. More important than GNP is the way income is distributed among the people as a whole. It is said that incomes have been equalized more than at any time before or after the war: however, those left behind by a growing economy must still not be forgotten. Even if rising per capita income in the world order should be delayed, it is more important that the well-being of these people should be provided for. Before we rejoiced over third place in GNP, we should have noted that even though the per capita income had tripled in less than 10 years and had risen to $1,122, personal consumption expenditures were only $733. The same might still be said of the 1979 per capita income of $6,300.

Even though gross national product may have risen and national income increased, if the stock of social capital in the living environment is inadequate, this increased wealth is that of the *nouveaux riches*. Such people are still poor compared to established families with old invested riches who may not, however, have cash on hand. In other words, even though there has been a sudden increase in income and a precipitous rise in level of consumption, if one has been poor he cannot soon attain the level of a wealthy man in standards of living. A sudden rise in the level of consumption produces an unbalanced life; the more rapid the rise, the greater the contradictions in one's life. Though materially rich, a man may become spiritually poor. And that is precisely what Japan is.

There is no need to consign GNP to hell, nor should efforts to raise it be abandoned, but worship of GNP must come to an end. For human beings and for society there are more important things—social welfare—for which the GNP must be used. In order that the welfare of society may be seen as objectively as possible and presented in a form that most people can understand, social welfare indicators should be established. The goal of raising these indicators should replace that of an increase in GNP. Japan could take pride in a high rate of "welfare growth" according to these indicators even if the increase of the GNP were to slow down.

2. From the Economic Superpower to a "Welfare Power"

Håkan Hedberg, the Swedish economic journalist who in 1969 wrote *The Challenge of Japan—the Economic Super-Power of the 1980s*, called Japan's economic growth the development of "heavyweight" industry in a "flyweight" country: "It's like a big *sumo* wrestler putting on tiny, very tiny, ballet slippers and dancing. Herein lies Japan's tragedy."

It has been estimated that the development of "heavyweight" industry, by a growth rate of 10 percent or more a year, would have raised the national income of the Japanese people in 1975 to 1.8 times what it was in 1970 and in 1980 to four times. Considering a growth rate in those days of 4.5 percent for the leading Western European countries and about 1.5 percent for America, Japan would have certainly reached the level of western Europe in the 1970s and by 1985 would overtake America. Because this forecast was made before the "dollar shock" and the upward revaluation of the yen, and the 1971 slump and the minus growth since the 1973 oil crisis did not enter into the calculations, an estimate now might be somewhat lower, but in any case this is phenomenal speed. I wonder if it is actually a good thing for the Japanese people to rush along this road to economic superpowerdom. With the recent economic recession, this daydream weakened, but who can say that the desire for stable growth will never be turned again toward rapid growth?

To plunge forward for economic power will only be a confirmation of the greedy "economic animal" image of Japanese and of the criticism by Asian countries that Japan is substituting economic for military agression. For Japan itself, pursuit of GNP could ultimately destroy any remaining humanity in life in Japan. Supposing Japan did surpass America in ten years—it would be a country with polluted air and contaminated water, in such a pitiful state that it could not guarantee the health of future generations. What would economic development do for Japan then? Even if the national income reached the American level, unequal distribution would still plague a whole group of people worried about their livelihood. Their anxiety would be all the greater if the rest of the country were prosperous. Even those free from anxiety would find it impossible to have adequate housing if land prices continue to rise. Though a great economic power might become an economic superpower, would it be a nation worthy of that name?

The dream must be completely abandoned now. The Japanese people were carried away all through the sixties with economics and production, but they should meet the challenge of the upcoming eighties by battling for society and better living conditions. They must bid farewell to the "production first" philosophy of the sixties and make their goal the restoration of human life. If there has never since the Meiji period been emphasis on restoring human life, let the eighties be the era in which this is established. If we could go back to the starting point of August 15, 1945, we should have laid our course at that point.

The level of social welfare must rise even at the sacrifice of growth in the economy. This is the era when equitable division of the pie should be put ahead of making the pie larger, when preservation and improvement of the environment and adequate development of social security should be emphasized over economic development. The aggravation of the contradictions which economic growth has brought us is now felt by the entire population, as even the prime minister admitted when he said: "There can be no growth without welfare." Times are indeed changing.

However, there is little room for optimism. Despite the destructive imbalance between economic and social development, the present system still places emphasis on the amount of return from investment. Expenditures for social welfare, which do not produce material benefits and are not directly connected with increasing production capacity, are made reluctantly. This has been the traditional course always followed by Japan. To overcome the lack of concern and awareness implicit in the traditional course is the only hope of building a society to be proud of.

Social welfare must consider the few hopelessly poor, the handful of the aged and the small number of disabled as problems of the people as a whole, not as problems for charity. It must become possible for everybody to grow into old age without being sorry to have lived so long; for families who through misfortune have become fatherless to live without hardship; and for the mentally and physically handicapped to live decent lives. Japan must become a society which truly guarantees to everyone, whether he can work to his fullest capacity or is unable to work, "a healthy and cultured life."

3. A Nation Great in Education and Learning

Despite the fact that Japan has universal compulsory education and is second only to America in the number of students receiving higher education, education—a "pillar" of social development—is also one problem of social development.

I have already pointed out how the rapid spread of education contributed to the modernization of Japan. We should reflect now on the proportion of their scanty wealth our Meiji predecessors spent on education. At the same time we should also thoroughly reconsider the kind of education provided since the time of Meiji, an education which produced loyal subjects who devoted their lives to the policy of national wealth and military strength.

First of all, Japan should actively increase investment in education. If the same proportion of wealth as that spent in the Meiji period were invested in education today, our elementary and secondary school system would improve to almost beyond recognition. No longer would our universities lack essential facilities. Secondly, the person who "builds" people should get preferential treatment over the one who builds things, and incentives for highly talented people to become teachers would make Japan a country great in education. Such a country would be worthy of more respect than one great in military power. Finally, the transfer of expenditures from military forces to education would produce a country great in peace.

Physical facilities for education and favorable conditions for teachers are not, however, in themselves sufficient for the development of men. If there is a lesson to be learned from education since the Meiji period it is that education must produce, not subjects, but citizens—citizens with an awareness of basic human rights who will critically watch developments in society and oppose any tendency to ignore or oppress men. "Respect for man" can be preached by those who do not, in fact, respect men; education must produce men who can see through such preaching. In education live the basic principles of democracy; Japan's democratic education should be carried out in fidelity to the spirit of the Basic Law on Education. In fact, however, postwar democratic education has been subjected to a reactionary distortion. Education in social studies has slipped back toward the old training in morality that it was supposed to replace. The man produced by such an education, while he may be well fitted to the morality of a great power, is certainly not the man to point the way to a nation great in social welfare. Indeed, what this kind of education produces is, on the one hand, a mass of men who selfishly conform, and, on the other, men who seek to escape society or to oppose it, not in constructive but in destructive ways.

If the decade of the eighties is to witness the founding of a new style of life in Japan, first, we must return to the starting point of the new education immediately following the war and reform the reactionary policies which have developed since that time; and second, through investment in education we must sweep away the disgrace of our educational poverty and turn Japan into a great cultural and educational nation. Some movement toward that goal has appeared in present educational reform; of the former, however, there has been not a sign. Yet only when the importance of policy reform is clearly understood will there be a correct understanding of the need for, and a truly effective use of, educational investment. Evil influences caused by the so-called *gakureki shakai* (credential society) which have recently come to the fore will not be corrected unless a new educational system is established along with reform of the society itself.

Reform of education is closely linked to the problem of academic freedom. So long as this freedom is not respected, no amount of improvement in physical educational facilities will create centers of learning. The campus disputes of 1968-69 represent the younger generation's rebellion against the present conditions of research and education. Unfortunately, this rebellion has not borne fruit; yet the lessons it taught must not be forgotten. While the rebellion did not have a clearly defined direction, it did pose fundamental questions about the meaning of scholarship, the significance of research, and the nature of education. It is for this reason that it had an impact on the entire country. The questions, moreover, were not directed at research and education alone; they sought to criticize the very society standing behind the educational system. This should not be treated lightly merely because of the destructive activities during the disputes or the decadence which later affected the student movement. Any real response to the questions raised by this rebellion demands that we preserve an unrestricted and genuine academic freedom.

Scholarship by its very nature transcends national boundaries. If Japan is to become a country in which scholarship is respected, then we must demand the development of a system appropriate to its national power to provide for international academic exchange. Japan may have become an economic giant, but in the academic field it remains a midget. Yet it is precisely in the academic field that it ought to become great, and toward this end it ought at least to provide the kind of financial backing that would allow this country to assume an academic role commensurate with its economic position. Exchange of scholars is little more substantial than it was in the period of reconstruction following the war, and, while the program for foreign students in Japan has broadened somewhat, it remains limited and the students' treatment remains poor. The poverty of Japan's programs in this area clearly testifies to the imbalance between an economic giant and an academic midget. Rectifying the imbalance demands a sharp increase in the kind of financial outlay that goes beyond simple material gain.

To carry out such a program of educational reform would be to turn Japan into a truly cultural nation. Such a Japan would allay the fears of other Asian countries and command the respect of the world. If it were to grow into such a nation there would surely be no need to strengthen a military force whose only *raison d'etre* is defense of the country. In Article 9 of their Constitution the Japanese people declared their renunciation of war; now they and their leaders must live up to that declaration. In the world of tomorrow it will be this quality that will prove Japan is an "advanced" country in the true sense of the term.

Index